UNDER THE GOLDEN DOME

UNDER THE GOLDEN DOME

Historic Talks and Tales from the
Massachusetts State House

Vol. I

Josh S. Cutler

For Mom

CONTENTS

Acknowledgments

1   Out with the old, in with the new (1798)   Pg 13

2   The gerrymander is born (1812)   Pg 18

3   Abolitionist trailblazer Angelina Grimké (1838)   Pg 22

4   Dorothea Dix: mental health crusader (1843)   Pg 26

5   The return of Sumner (1856)   Pg 31

6   The status and statues of Daniel Webster (1859)   Pg 34

7   The British invasion (1860)   Pg 37

8   Governor Andrew and the return of the colors (1865)   Pg 41

9   Pioneering lawmakers sworn in (1867)   Pg 44

10   A Mashpee farmer makes history (1886)   Pg 49

11   Young Helen Keller shares a vision for change (1903)   Pg 52

12   Roosevelt takes on his protégé (1912)   Pg 56

13   Taft strikes back (1912)   Pg 61

14   The faith of Calvin Coolidge (1914)   Pg 66

15	The Suffragists and the President (1919)	Pg 72
16	Veteran visits for the ages (1924)	Pg 75
17	Madame Speaker (1926)	Pg 78
18	A Lincoln likeness (1928)	Pg 86
19	A revolutionary tercentenary (1930)	Pg 88
20	'Flying daughter' welcomed home (1932)	Pg 95
21	The case of the Cod Caper (1933)	Pg 100
22	A loyalty oath (1935)	Pg 107
23	Bringing down the House—and Senate! (1937)	Pg 109
24	War time measures (1942)	Pg 112
25	Taxing policies (1947)	Pg 114
26	Douglas MacArthur returns (1951)	Pg 116
27	The lone walk (1953)	Pg 121
28	A 'flood of filth' (1954)	Pg 128
29	Hearst warns of 'Red Menace' (1955)	Pg 130
30	Gleason plays bit part in beano brouhaha (1959)	Pg 134
31	John F. Kennedy's city on a hill (1961)	Pg 137
32	Reverend King stirs and inspires (1965)	Pg 144
33	Veep visit validates Volpe (1968)	Pg 150
34	Student protesters swarm State House (1970)	Pg 153
	Note on sources	Pg 157
	Selected bibliography	Pg 159
	Index	Pg 162
	Endnotes	Pg 165
	About the author	Pg 175

ACKNOWLEDGMENTS

I spent over a decade walking the halls of the Massachusetts State House, gathering bits of history along the way—stories from veteran colleagues and staff, insights from the delightful Doric Docent tours, or just through serendipitous encounters with the portraits, statues, and murals that line the corridors. Yet, I must confess that despite all my years working at the State House, I never truly paused to appreciate the depth and significance of events that have unfolded within these walls. It is cliché that we often take for granted what is right in front of us. This book is an attempt to remedy that.

I've had a blast tackling this project and delving into some well-known and lesser-known historical events at the State House. Each event has a story, and I hope you enjoy learning about them as much as I've enjoyed writing about them. Balancing the significance of various events and deciding which to include was perhaps my biggest challenge. I ultimately chose to focus on events that occurred before 1970—a somewhat arbitrary cutoff, to be sure—but as astute readers will note, this work is ambitiously titled "Volume I." I welcome any feedback or suggestions for inclusion in a future Volume II.

This project is a bit of a departure from my two previous publications, which I will take a moment to plug here: The *Boston Gentlemen's Mob*, focused on the fateful abolition riot of 1835, and *Mobtown Massacre*, which recounts a War of 1812-era incident when the free press had to be defended by muskets.

As before, I want to thank my team of beta readers who offered feedback, edits, and suggestions at different steps of this process. Grateful appreciation to Tom O'Brien, Smitty Pignatelli, Ruth Balser, Kathy LaNatra, Norman Sabbey, and Jim Cantwell. Thank you also to House Clerk Steven James, a font of historical information himself, for his encouragement and support.

Researching this book—tracking down newspaper clippings, journals, images, and other archival materials—was made much easier with the help of a number of individuals. Thank you to Susanna Coit, archivist and research library assistant, Perkins School for the Blind; April Pascucci, legislative reference librarian, State Library of Massachusetts; Donna Russo, library and archive specialist, Historic New England; Kirstin Kay, archivist, UMass Special Collections and University Archives; Nathan Sowry, reference archivist, Smithsonian; and Eleanor Giller, head of rights & reproductions, New York Historical Society.

I would also like to acknowledge the Wethersfield Historical Society, the Massachusetts Secretary of State, Boston Public Library, Massachusetts Historical Society, and the Massachusetts Trial Court Law Libraries.

Thank you to Lori for all the love and support.

THE MASSACHUSETTS STATE HOUSE

c 1827

1858

1875

1899

c.1900-1910

1965

*Images courtesy of the Boston Public Library, Library of Congress,
State House Library, and Peabody Essex Museum.*

OUT WITH THE OLD, IN WITH THE NEW (1798)

*In this House, may the true principles of the best
system of civil government the world has ever seen,
be uniformly supported.*

JANUARY 11, 1798: When Governor Increase Sumner arrived at noon in the Senate chamber, it signaled the end of an era for the Massachusetts state capitol. The historic building, site of the Boston Massacre and seat of state government since the American Revolution, would henceforth be known as the Old State House.

Once the legislature had adjourned their cramped and poorly ventilated quarters for a final time, Governor Sumner led the march to their larger, modern, and "most magnificent" new edifice a short distance away on Beacon Hill. Designed by architect Charles Bulfinch, the new red brick State House was located on a piece of land that was once the late Governor John Hancock's cow pasture.

State House Library.

Governor Sumner.

An extensive coterie of state officers and militia leaders trailed behind Governor Sumner in a triumphant procession. They included the lieutenant governor, executive council, state secretary, treasurer, and chaplain, along with more than two hundred senators and representatives and their clerks. Spectators lined the route to observe while drum and fife music filled the air. The rich aroma of West Indian rum and exotic coffees and sugars wafted from the wharf at the other end of State Street, where a new cargo ship had just arrived in port.[1]

The venerable parade proceeded up along Beacon Street toward the arcaded entrance of the new State House, which had been under construction for the past two-and-a-half years. The cornerstone was first laid on July 4, 1795, drawn by fifteen white horses to symbolize the fifteen states in the union. Paul Revere and Governor Samuel Adams presided over the ceremony.

Governor Adams had stepped down after four years in office and was now succeeded by Sumner, a fifty-one-year-old Federalist and former Supreme Judicial Court justice. Governor Sumner represented a younger generation of leaders in Massachusetts and remained a popular figure, known for his amiable nature and urbane manner.

He led the procession inside the building through a large entry hall filled with two rows of Doric columns and then to the new Representatives Hall on the upper story. The chambers for the senate and the executive council were located on either side.

The original State House dome was made of wooden shingles. In 1802, the dome was sheathed with over six thousand feet of rolled copper by Paul Revere's foundry. The dome was painted yellow in 1831, and gold-leaf was added in 1874. *Boston Public Library*.

Above, a wooden dome with gray shingles, some thirty-feet high and fifty-feet in diameter, crowned the room. A gilded wooden pinecone sat atop the exterior cupola to represent one of the commonwealth's key staples.

In addition to the three main chambers, the building featured about two dozen smaller and plainer offices for committee use.[2]

The stately new building, elevated above Boston Harbor, offered striking vistas, and vied "with the most picturesque scenes in Europe," according to one observer.[3]

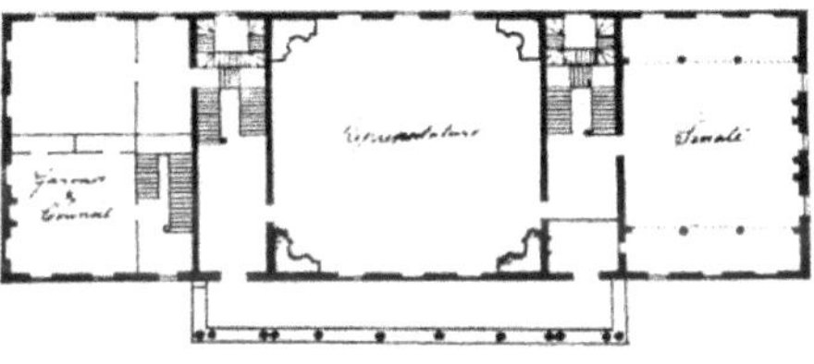

State House Library.

After a moment of pause and official blessing, Reverend Peter Thacher offered a "peculiarly elegant and pertinent" prayer to formally dedicate the building. Following the brief ceremony, the parties withdrew to their appropriate chambers and the House commenced its first official business in the new State House. By three o'clock that afternoon their inaugural session was adjourned.

The following morning Governor Sumner returned to offer formal remarks to both branches of the legislature. In his speech he offered praise to the new State House, calling it a monument to the public spirit of the citizens of Massachusetts.

"In this House, may the true principles of the best system of civil government the world has ever seen, be uniformly supported. Here, may every practice and principle be successfully opposed, that tend to impair it. Here may every act of the Legislature be the result of cool deliberation and sound judgment. And in this House, on all necessary occasions, may the Supreme Executive, agreeably to the laws of the land, in mercy cause judgment to be executed. And each branch of our elective government, continuing faithful discharge of its trust, God grant, that neither external force or influence, nor internal commotion or violence, may ever shake the pillars of our free Republic."[4]

Sumner also shared an update on the state's fiscal health and used part of his speech to weigh in on the ongoing conflict in Europe, warning of the dangers posed to the nation's trade interests by the new French Republic. The House and Senate later followed up with their own formal responses to the governor's inaugural remarks. Both branches shared praise for the new capitol.

"We sincerely rejoice with you and our fellow citizens at large on the completion of this public edifice, combining elegance with utility and constituting a distinguished ornament of the metropolis, whose inhabitants generously provided the place on which it is erected," the Senate declared.[5]

The House added: "Long may it continue an ornament to the Capital, whose inhabitants generously gave the situation on which it is erected, and a monument of the public spirit of the people of Massachusetts, sacred to the purpose to which it has been devoted."[6]

Once the formalities were concluded, the two branches returned to their normal session schedule, though there were still some details of the new building that needed tending to. The Senate decided that a carpet was necessary for their chamber and voted to procure one, while the lower branch sought changes to the heating system so as to "give more warmth to the House."[7]

One of the earliest photographs of the State House in 1858 shows the Bulfinch design and original cupola before major renovations were made in the 1860s. *Boston Public Library*.

Thursday Jan. 11, 1798. 113

The original Senate Journal of January 11, 1798, reports on the transition to the new State House. *State Library of Massachusetts*

THE GERRYMANDER IS BORN (1812)

*The Doctor has decreed that this monster
shall be denominated a Gerry-mander*

FEBRUARY 11, 1812: The bevy of new bills landing on Governor Elbridge Gerry's desk in early February included a controversial measure to regulate the treatment of mischievous dogs, but it was political mischief that was on the minds of many.

The Massachusetts House and Senate had just enacted a bill to reapportion state legislative districts, a seemingly mundane process necessitated each decade, but one steeped with political overtones. Though the state boasted a strong Federalist presence, the Republican Party had recently won control of both chambers and its leaders wanted to preserve their narrow majority by drawing favorable voting districts for the next election.[8]

The tradition was not new. Manipulating politically advantageous legislative districts was a practice that had existed in some form for centuries––dating back at least to the British borough system.[9] What was perhaps new was the brazen manner in which the Massachusetts legislature had undertaken to accomplish it. Their plan drew a highly partisan state senate map that carved up existing county lines, which had traditionally served as district boundaries. The result was the creation of several new oddly-shaped districts.

The most egregious outcome was north of Boston in Essex County, where Governor Gerry hailed from. It was traditionally a staunchly Federalist region, but legislative leaders creatively packed several pro-Federalist towns together to enlarge their own Republican majorities in the rest of the county. The result was that a region that would have normally elected a delegation of five Federalists, was now expected to give the Republicans a three-to-two advantage.

The Federalists immediately cried foul. The Republican redistricting plan would "shake the foundation of our republic," they argued, and drafted a lengthy statement of protest signed by more than two hundred state lawmakers.[10] The message was widely published in the local press.

Governor Elbridge Gerry lost his re-election bid in 1812 but was later picked to serve as vice president to President James Madison. *Boston Public Library.*

"We feel, and cannot but express, a serious alarm at the nature and consequences of this measure," they wrote. "Free governments … have fallen a prey to the ambition and to the lust of dominion, of a few individuals. We hope, that such an awful catastrophe is not to be visited upon us, in the infancy of our republic."[11]

Governor Gerry, a signer of the Declaration of Independence and former member of the Continental Congress, counted himself a loyal Jeffersonian Republican. He was mistrustful of the Federalists and not eager to see them return to power in Massachusetts, so he signed the redistricting measure into law—reluctantly, according to some accounts.

Whether they considered him the driving force or not, Federalists were eager to pin the blame on Governor Gerry and turn the episode to their own political advantage. The following month a pro-Federalist newspaper published a cartoon depicting the oddly-shaped Essex based district as "a

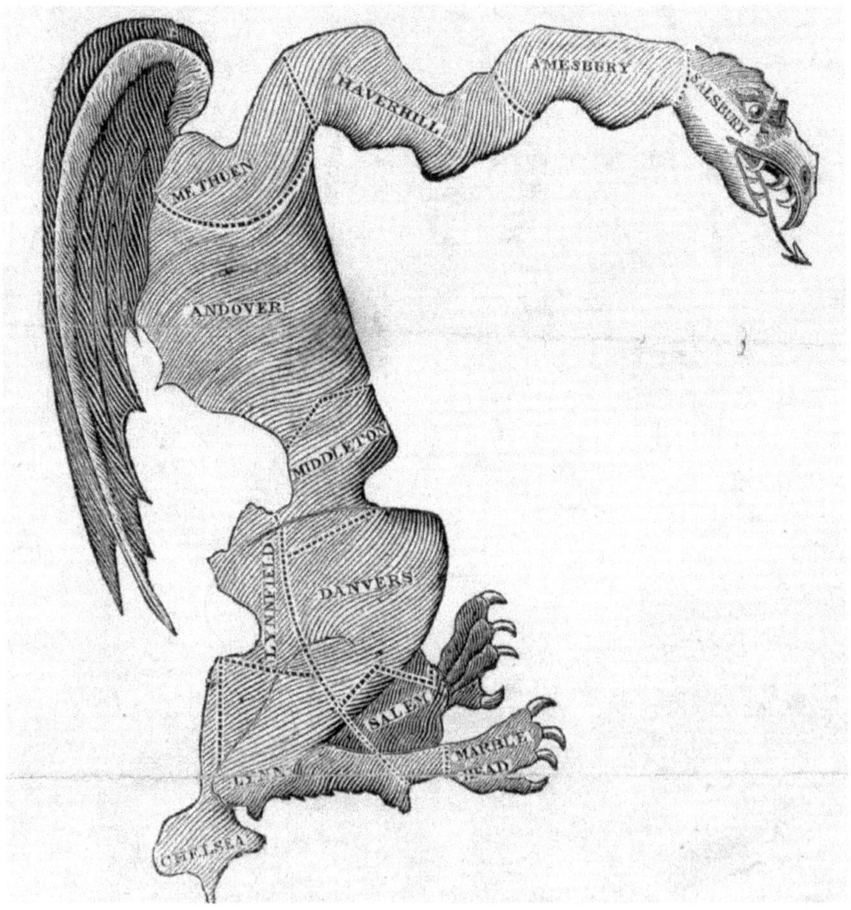

The "Gerrymander" first appeared in the *Boston Gazette* on March 27, 1812, and then a day later in the *Boston Repertory & General Advertiser*. *Boston Public Library.*

new species of Monster" resembling a salamander, accented with hand-drawn head, claws and wings.[12]

A lengthy editorial accompanied the cartoon, sarcastically detailing the taxonomy of the new species with credit to Governor Gerry for its creation. "The Doctor has decreed that this monster shall be denominated a Gerry-mander, a name that must exceedingly gratify the parental bosom of our worthy Chief Magistrate, and prove so highly flattering to his ambition," the paper wrote.[13]

The Gerry-mander was born.

There are conflicting accounts as to the author of the drawing, but regardless of its origin, the newly coined term was quickly embraced and widely replicated across the state. Within a few months the term "Gerrymander" (soon just "gerrymander") was appearing in newspapers around the nation.

The controversy, along with a brewing war with Great Britain, contributed to the narrow defeat of Governor Gerry in his re-election bid that spring. The Federalist Party rebounded in Massachusetts and recaptured both the governor's office and the state House of Representatives. The gerrymander proved a remarkably effective tool, however — even in the face of a Federalist surge, the Republican Party maintained its grip on the state Senate by a two-to-one margin.

For Governor Gerry, his term of office had ended, but his eponymous legacy would prove long lasting.

Chapter 3

ABOLITIONIST TRAILBLAZER ANGELINA GRIMKÉ (1838)

*We Abolition Women are
turning the world upside down.*

FEBRUARY 21, 1838: Underneath the yellow copper State House dome that still leaked rain and snow on occasion a plainly dressed woman in a Quaker hat with a Southern drawl was about to make history.

Thirty-three-year-old Angelina Grimké stood by the speaker's desk in Representatives Hall and surveyed the chamber.[14] Every seat was filled, and the galleries, lobby, and hallways were crammed with guests—including a handful of Black faces. The House and Senate members of the Joint Committee on Slavery sat arrayed in front of her, flanked by security. All were eagerly waiting for the noted abolitionist and women's suffrage advocate to speak.

The crowd began arriving more than an hour ahead of time and comprised some of Boston's most prominent residents. Many others had travelled from across the state, including from Worcester, Plymouth, Lowell, and Weymouth. Some were turned away at the door. Although no formal notice was given, it was widely known that the South Carolina native was to address the legislature on this Wednesday afternoon in February.

Grimké felt her heart beating and tried to steady her nerves. Though she was by now an experienced speaker, this was no ordinary lecture. No woman had ever publicly addressed a legislative body in the nation before and the momentous nature of the day's event was clearly evident. She later acknowledged to a friend that she felt the weight of this "tremendous hour."[15]

"Mr. Chairman, more than two thousand years have rolled their dark and bloody waters down the rocky,

Angelina Grimké. *Library of Congress.*

winding channel of time into the broad ocean of eternity since woman's voice was heard in the palace of an eastern monarch...," she began.[16]

"I stand before you as a citizen, on behalf of the twenty thousand women of Massachusetts, whose names are enrolled on petitions which have been submitted to the legislature of which you are the organ," she told the committee. "These petitions relate to the great and solemn subject of American slavery—a subject fraught with the deepest interest to this republic, whether we regard it in its political, moral, or religious aspects."

Once her speech was underway, Grimké's posture relaxed and her confidence grew. Despite her diminutive stature and plain appearance, she was a powerful and eloquent orator. "Her voice was melodious, and her manner of delivery quite pleasing," noted one observer.[17] Maria Weston Chapman, a leader in the growing Boston abolitionist movement, was even more effusive, calling her speech "lucid, weighty, ... and powerfully driven home."[18]

The vast majority of the audience members listened respectfully and attentively, though Grimké's remarks drew a few hisses in some corners of the room. It seemed that not all shared her views on slavery, nor approved of a woman speaking out in public.

Grimké and her older sister Sarah had grown up on a Southern plantation in Charleston and the cruelties they witnessed inflicted upon enslaved persons had left an indelible impact. The sisters later moved to Philadelphia where they joined the Quaker faith and became active in the anti-slavery cause.

Grimké soon made the acquaintance of William Lloyd Garrison, editor of the radical abolitionist newspaper, the *Liberator*, and later penned a pamphlet appealing to Southern women to speak out against slavery. The efforts helped to launch her career as an abolitionist writer and speaker and led to a series of lectures across the northeast. Some of her meetings were before a mixed crowd of women and men, which further rankled those who felt she was engaged in "unwomanly behavior."

Her speech to the Massachusetts legislature came about following a signature drive campaign advocating for an end to slavery in Washington, D.C. Prominent Boston abolitionists suggested that Grimké present the signatures to the legislature's Committee on Slavery and the committee chairman readily agreed.

Sarah Grimké. *Library of Congress.*

Grimké's persuasive anti-slavery oratory and the added credibility she brought as a native Southerner made her ideally suited to the cause. Her sister Sarah had also been scheduled to join her, but she came down with a bad cold and was unable to attend.

"I stand before you as a Southerner, exiled from the land of my birth, by the sound of the lash, and the pitious cry of the slave," she told the committee, recalling her childhood in South Carolina. "I stand before you as a repentant slaveholder."

Grimké was an advocate for the immediate emancipation of all enslaved persons, which put her at odds with even some Northern abolition advocates who backed a more gradual approach to ending slavery.

She also did not shy away from what some called the "woman question." Grimké was determined to lift up the cause of women's suffrage along with her anti-slavery message. "Are we aliens because we are women? Are we bereft of citizenship, because we are the mothers, wives, and daughters of a mighty people?" she asked the audience.

"I hold, Mr. Chairman, that American women have to do with this subject, not only because it is moral and religious, but because it is political, inasmuch as we are citizens of this republic, and as such, our honor, happiness, and well-being, are bound up in its politics, government and laws."

Her speech kept the audience's rapt attention for more than two hours. By the time the shadows had fully enveloped the State House dome she concluded her remarks for the day. Grimké still had more to say, however, and plans were made for her to return two days later.

She spoke before another packed room on Friday afternoon for over two hours and finally capped off her address with a third visit one week later. In all, Grimké spoke for more than six hours over the course of three days.[19]

Coverage of the event in the Boston press was mixed, breaking down along expected ideological grounds. The more established newspapers mostly offered derisive commentary or else ignored the significance of the event altogether.

The *Liberator* lavished praise on Grimké's speech and republished excerpts. Another progressive Boston paper declared it "a noble day when for the first time in civilized America, a woman stood up in a Legislative Hall, vindicating the rights of women."[20]

For her own part Grimké could be a tough self-critic, but she was pleased by her performance and the response to her speech. It would be another eighty years before women earned the right to vote and even longer before a woman would serve in the Massachusetts legislature, or even be allowed to sit in the House chamber, but Grimké knew something important had just occurred.

In a letter written to a friend soon after her speech she declared, "We Abolition Women are turning the world upside down."[21]

Chapter 4

DOROTHEA DIX: MENTAL HEALTH CRUSADER (1843)

*I come to place before the Legislature of
Massachusetts the condition of the miserable,
the desolate, the outcast.*

JANUARY 19, 1843: Dorothea Dix didn't expect to become a national crusader when she first visited an East Cambridge jail for a Sunday school class.

Inside, she was shocked to find mentally ill women imprisoned in a bare stone cell without basic necessities like heat, their teeth chattering in the cold. The squalid scene left an enduring memory. When the local jailer refused to take any steps to remedy the situation, Dix spoke up. She helped bring the issue to the attention of county officials who eventually relented and approved the addition of new stoves to warm the cells.

It was a modest victory, but Dix nonetheless felt empowered. She was also determined to do more. The thirty-nine-year-old schoolteacher spent the next two years touring jails, asylums, and almshouses across the state to document the treatment of the mentally ill. She filled her journal with painful observations of the neglect and abuse she witnessed at dozens of facilities from Wellfleet to Newburyport to Springfield.

By the winter of 1843, Dix was ready to take the next step. She enlisted help from an influential network of like-minded reformers, including Dr.

Samuel Gridley Howe, a state legislator and advocate for the disabled, and a young attorney named Charles Sumner. Her goal was to present her findings to the legislature and help secure funding for services to aid the mentally ill.

Dix carefully drafted a report laying out the facts over thirty-two pages and nearly fifteen thousand words. As a woman, she knew that she would not likely be permitted to address legislators directly in person, so she arranged for her remarks to be filed as a petition in the Massachusetts House of Representatives.

The petition, entitled a Memorial to the Massachusetts Legislature, was formally presented on Thursday, January 19, 1843, and referred to the Committee on Public Charitable Institutions. Dix had collected

Dorothea Dix's petition to the legislature in 1843 was the start of a lifelong crusade to improve care of the mentally ill. Her advocacy led to widespread reforms and the creation of dozens of new state mental hospitals across the country. *Library of Congress.*

copious notes to document her observations and warned legislators that her findings were "displeasing, coarse, and severe."[22]

"I come to present the strong claims of suffering humanity. I come to place before the legislature of Massachusetts the condition of the miserable, the desolate, the outcast," she wrote. "If I inflict pain upon you, and move you to horror, it is to acquaint you with sufferings which you have the power to alleviate, and make you hasten to the relief of the victims of legalized barbarity."

Dix took care not to place all the blame with local wardens and jailkeepers. They were not acting out of willful cruelty, she explained, but oftentimes ignorance and a lack of training or resources. "Familiarity with suffering, it is said, blunts the sensibilities, and where neglect once finds a footing, other injuries are multiplied," she wrote.

She argued that jails and almshouses were not designed to accommodate the needs of the mentally ill, and yet by law wardens were compelled to accept such patients, most of whom would be better served in a county hospital. Stronger laws were needed to make change which she hoped her observations would help spur.

"I proceed, gentlemen, briefly to call your attention to the present state of insane persons confined within this Commonwealth, in cages, closets, cellars, stalls, pens! Chained, naked, beaten with rods, and lashed into obedience!" she wrote.

Dix listed out all her various stops with descriptions of what she found. In some cases, she reported a brief summary, while in others she went into great detail with her observations.

Concord: A woman from the hospital in a cage in the almshouse.

Taunton: One woman caged.

Plymouth. One man stall-caged, from Worcester hospital.

Scituate. One man and one woman, stall-caged.

Dedham: two females in stalls, situated in the main building; lie in wooden bunks filled with straw; always shut up.

Granville. One often closely confined; now losing the use of his limbs from want of exercise.[23]

In Newburyport she toured an almshouse and visited a woman held in the cellar, over the protests of the house master. Dix described descending the stairs and hearing strange, unnatural noises. "But judge my horror and amazement, when a door to a closet beneath the staircase was opened, revealing in the imperfect light a female apparently wasted to a skeleton, partially wrapped in blankets, furnished for the narrow bed on which she was sitting; her countenance furrowed, not by age, but suffering, was the image of distress."[24]

The woman cried out in despair, asking why she was being held in the dark and forsaken. For Dix, the encounter left her chilled: "Those groans, those wailings come up daily, mingling, with how many others, a perpetual and sad memorial."

Dix described an October visit to an almshouse in Newton and seeing a lodging room filled with filthy straw. "The inmate herself was even more horribly repelling; she rushed out, as far as the chains would allow, almost in a state of nudity, exposed to a dozen persons, and vociferating at the top of her voice."[25]

Some of her encounters were more uplifting. To show how a kinder hand could lead to better outcomes for the mentally ill, Dix described a visit to the town of Barre, where the local practice was to have families care for the indigent in their homes in exchange for a small sum. There she met a family hosting a young woman who had previously been described as a "raving madwoman," but now appeared "well clothed, neat, quiet, and employed at needle-work."

The improved outcome was easy to diagnose. Instead of caging, or locking the woman up when she acted out, the family put a pair of mittens over her hands to prevent mischief, Dix recounted. "It is the same person; another family hold her in charge who better understand human nature and human influences," she wrote.

It was a lesson she hoped her legislative audience would also heed, and she concluded her lengthy report with a call for action. "Gentlemen, I commit to you this sacred cause. Your action upon this subject will affect the present and future condition of hundreds and of thousands."[26]

Dix's shocking findings had an immediate impact, though not everyone was pleased. Some local officials objected to the portrayal of their jails and almshouses, and, in many cases, she came under personal attack. In Danvers,

Dix served as superintendent of army nurses during the Civil War, helping to recruit hundreds of nurses to the Union cause and creating new opportunities for women in the nursing field. After the war she continued her work advocating for the disabled and the mentally ill. *Library of Congress.*

the Overseers of the Poor penned a lengthy statement to their local newspaper denying her findings.[27] "Bare-faced falsehoods, false impressions, and false statements," another letter writer wrote.[28]

Dr. Howe, Sumner and others defended Dix's report which, despite the objections, accomplished her goal of focusing attention on the plight of the mentally ill. Excerpts were published in area newspapers and captured the public's attention. The Legislature's Charitable Institutions Committee, chaired by Dr. Howe, promptly made a series of recommendations to the full body, including a major expansion of the state mental hospital. The funding was approved and Dix won a major victory.[29]

Fresh off the success with her Memorial to the Massachusetts Legislature, Dix was contacted by a clergy member in neighboring Rhode Island looking for help for a mentally ill inmate. Dix promptly set off in a stagecoach to Providence and thus began the next leg of what soon became a national crusade.

Over the next two decades she would crisscross the country in her quest to build more hospitals and improve the welfare of those grappling with mental illness, spurring widespread reforms. In her lobbying efforts she developed friendships with influential leaders like President Millard Fillmore and even travelled to Europe, where she once had an audience with the pope and successfully convinced him to improve conditions at the local asylum. During the Civil War, Dix served as a nurse and later continued her work as a humanitarian and social reformer until her death.

Though she was not even eligible to vote, Dorothea Dix had a major influence on public policy. Starting with her Memorial to the Massachusetts Legislature, Dix helped spark a national movement to change laws and attitudes about mental health.

Chapter 5

THE RETURN OF SUMNER
(1856)

I avoid no labor, I shrink from no exposure,
and complain of no hardship.

NOVEMBER **3, 1856:** A few months earlier, Charles Sumner had lain on the floor of the United States Senate, soaking in his own blood following a brutal attack from a pro-slavery South Carolina congressman. Now, Sumner paraded to the Massachusetts State House in an eleven-carriage procession, flanked by three militia divisions, with thousands of spectators waving American flags and cheering him on.

A gathering of thirty-one young women wearing wreaths and dressed in white stopped to present him with bouquets of flowers, while two brass

Senator Charles Sumner c. 1855.
Boston Public Library.

A depiction of the attack on Senator Charles Sumner by South Carolina Congressman Preston Brooks in May of 1856, two days after Sumner had delivered a blistering anti-slavery speech known as the "Crime Against Kansas" address. Brooks struck Sumner with a wooden cane repeatedly until it splintered, leaving Sumner unconscious in the Senate chamber. *Boston Public Library.*

bands filled the air with patriotic music. Near the corner of Shawmut Avenue, a line of flags and a banner colorfully proclaimed that "Massachusetts loves, honors, and will sustain her noble Senator."[30]

The elaborate procession began in Cambridge, where Sumner was staying, and wound through Brookline and Roxbury on its way to the State House. When the group arrived shortly before four o'clock, they were greeted by a vast assemblage in front of Beacon Street, estimated at more than fifteen thousand people. Others watched from the balconies and roofs of nearby buildings. Most local business had closed up shop for the afternoon and it seemed as if the entire city of Boston had turned out to welcome him.

The triumphal return marked Sumner's first public appearance since the attack. though he remained physically weak and had his doctor ride along with him in the carriage. The senator still felt the after-effects of the traumatic experience and sometimes took morphine in order to sleep. "My brain and whole nervous system are still jangled and subject to relapse," he wrote a friend one month prior.[31]

Governor Henry Gardner formally greeted Sumner in front of the State House, where a platform was set up for a reception. Gardner was joined by a coterie of state officials and his council. After some introductions, the governor offered brief remarks, praising Sumner as an orator, scholar, statesman, and "successful defender of [the country's] integrity and her honor."[32]

When Sumner rose and stepped from his carriage, his frailty was readily apparent. "His personal appearance showed the effect of severe physical suffering," one observer noted.[33] After the applause from the roaring crowd subsided, he launched into his own formal remarks.

Sumner had spoken for only a minute or two when he faltered—and could not continue. "My voice and my strength will not permit," he informed the audience and handed off the remainder of his written remarks to reporters. The remainder of his speech was later published in the *Liberator* and other Boston newspapers.

In his written address, Sumner acknowledged that he still felt the aftereffects from the assault but made clear he would not yield in his fight against slavery:

> *"In all simplicity let me say I seek nothing but the triumph of truth. … Show me that I am wrong, and I stop at once; but in the complete conviction of right I shall persevere against all temptation, against all odds, against all threats—knowing well that whatever may be my fate, the right will surely prevail."*

Sumner's speech concluded with a pledge: "I avoid no labor, I shrink from no exposure, and complain of no hardship." Afterwards, he returned to his carriage and was escorted home while the band played "Sweet Home.

News of Sumner's return to the State House was covered widely in the press. The brutal attack in May had shocked the consciousness of many and engendered sympathy across Massachusetts, and much of the nation—though hard feelings remained in some parts. Sumner was known to be a strident and uncompromising abolitionist and many Southerners felt the attack was in some measure justified.

In a stark reminder of the sectional differences that divided the nation, a group of pro-Southern activists celebrating the election of President James Buchanan marched in Washington D.C. with a banner that read: "Sumner and Kansas—let 'em bleed."[34]

Chapter 6

THE STATUS
AND STATUES OF
DANIEL WEBSTER (1859)

*Where is fanaticism to find a stopping place in
Massachusetts, if it can proceed with impunity
beyond this disgraceful demonstration?*

SEPTEMBER 27, 1859: The
unveiling of an eight-foot statue
honoring the late Daniel
Webster drew a crowd of thousands to
the State House in the fall of 1859,
including former President Franklin
Pierce.[35] It also attracted a few critics
who would have preferred to cast
stones at the former senator rather
than memorialize him in bronze.

Webster, who also served as United
States Secretary of State, was known
for his eloquent oratory,
statesmanship, and legal acumen. To
many abolitionists, however, he was

Senator Daniel Webster.
Boston Public Library.

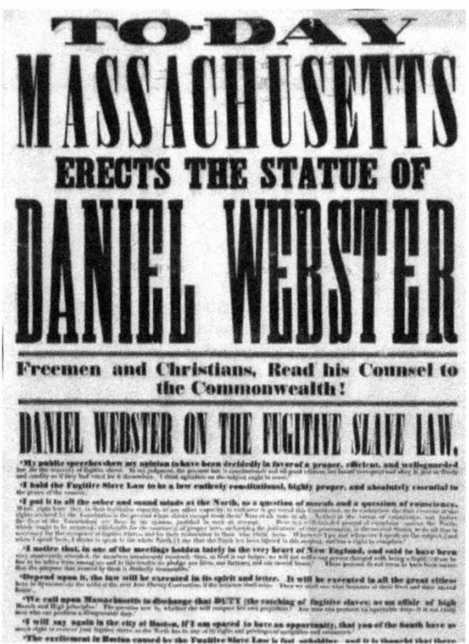

Abolitionists used this broadside to remind the public of Senator Webster's past statements in support of a controversial fugitive slave law. *Boston Public Library*

also known for compromising on a contentious fugitive slave law that expanded the power of Southern slaveholders to recapture runaway enslaved persons.

Webster had famously endorsed the Compromise of 1850 in a three-hour-plus speech known as his Seventh of March address. "Mr. President, I wish to speak today, not as a Massachusetts man, nor as a Northern man, but as an American, … I speak today for the preservation of the Union. 'Hear me for my cause,'" he declared.

Webster believed the proposals, which included admitting California as a free state and banning the trade of enslaved persons in Washington D.C., would help avert a civil war.

The compromise was deeply unpopular in New England, however, and Webster lost much of his support. He resigned his senate seat the following year and was ultimately replaced by Charles Sumner, a far more radical anti-slavery advocate. Webster continued his public career with a brief second stint as secretary of state, until his untimely death in 1852. Advocates, and some later historians, cast Webster's actions as an act of courage, sacrificing his political ambitions in an attempt to preserve the union.

The abolitionists, including *Liberator* newspaper publisher William Lloyd Garrison, never forgave Webster, however, and bitterly opposed his recognition. They immediately called for the statue to be removed, claiming it desecrated the grounds of the State House, and circulated a handbill reciting Webster's own words in support of the fugitive slave law. The *Liberator* also published pages of letters and commentary in opposition to the statue and petitions were signed asking for its removal.

"The Webster statue must be removed. This must be the special business of the next legislature, coupled with the act of making Massachusetts free to every hunted slave who seeks an asylum on her soil," the paper wrote.[36] The petition being circulated read:

"We the undersigned citizens of the Commonwealth of Massachusetts respectfully ask you to remove from the State House grounds—as no honor to the State and repugnant to the moral sense of the people—the statue of Daniel Webster, whose last years were spent in defending the Fugitive Slave Bill and whose last counsel to the Commonwealth was to 'conquer her prejudices' against slavehunting and to return men to bondage 'with alacrity.'"

Webster still had plenty of defenders and many felt that the abolitionist tactics were disrespectful—including the circulation of petitions among the crowd during the unveiling ceremony. One newspaper likened the push to remove Webster's statue to the demolition of Bunker Hill Monument, or the Washington Monument (which was still in construction in the nation's capital). "Where is fanaticism to find a stopping place in Massachusetts, if it can proceed with impunity beyond this disgraceful demonstration?"[37]

The fugitive slave law was eventually repealed by Congress at the end of the Civil War. The Webster statue remained.

The dedication of a statue to the late Daniel Webster in the fall of 1859 drew thousands to the State House, including a few unhappy abolitionists who objected to the tribute and tried to have the statue removed – unsuccessfully. *Boston Public Library.*

Chapter 7

THE BRITISH INVASION
(1860)

*I hear so much in praise of the Prince of Wales
that I fear the people will all turn Royalists.*

OCTOBER 18, 1860: The Massachusetts State House looked more akin to the British House of Lords for a brief time in the fall of 1860, with the arrival of Prince Albert Edward and his royal party from the United Kingdom. The young Prince of Wales, eldest son of Queen Victoria, made the historic visit as part of a nationwide goodwill tour, becoming the first heir to the British throne to visit the United States.

Governor Nathaniel Banks and a multitude of public officials greeted the nineteen-year-old in princely style during his Boston sojourn. Following an elaborate parade before throngs of cheering well-wishers, the prince arrived at the State House on a Thursday afternoon, dressed in his formal British army attire with a plumed chapeau. The royal visit was observed as a public holiday; children were given a day off from school and most businesses closed by noon.

The prince was escorted into the State House through Doric Hall and then formally introduced in the Governor's Council chamber, which had been outfitted in majestic style for the reception. The chamber ante-rooms were decorated with royal purple and gold fringe, with the traditional arms of England and shield of Massachusetts on display. Several historical keepsakes were laid out in the governor's room to mark the occasion, including a twelfth century bible transcript, a copy of the Massachusetts Bay province charter, a witchcraft manuscript, and the Oxford address on the ascension of King George III.

"It is with great pleasure that I welcome your Royal Highness to the Commonwealth of Massachusetts and extend to you the most cordial greetings of its people," declared Governor Banks in his brief welcoming remarks. "They have regarded with profound gratification your visit to this continent, so auspicious in its opening, so fortunate in its progress."[38]

The governor led the prince and his royal retinue, which included assorted dukes, earls, and lords, to the Senate chamber and then to Representatives Hall, where he offered a brief explanation of the role of each branch and the nature of legislative committees. The prince bowed in response but did not offer any formal remarks during his brief tour, which by most accounts lasted about twenty minutes.

The royal procession departed via the west exit of the State House where their horses were waiting. Prince Albert Edward mounted his steed, the "Black Prince," and joined Governor Banks and other dignitaries for a military display on the Boston Common with the Ancient and Honorable Artillery Company and more than three thousand troops.

Prince Albert Edward, eldest son of Queen Victoria, visited the State House in 1860 as a teenager while on a North American goodwill tour. Four decades later he ascended to the British throne as King Edward VII. *Royal Collection Trust.*

Afterwards, the prince and his guests returned to the State House for a collation, where they were joined by Senator Charles Sumner, Senator Henry Wilson and top legislative, military, and judicial leaders. The day's elaborate festivities concluded that evening with a formal ball at the Academy of Music, which featured a sixty-person orchestra and a musical chorus led by twelve hundred school children singing "God Save the Queen."[39]

Revolutionary War veteran Ralph Farnum fought against the rule of King George III and later shook hands with his great-great-grandson, the Prince of Wales, during a Royal visit to Boston. *Massachusetts Historical Society.*

The most memorable event of the crown prince's historic visit to Boston, however, may have been a brief encounter earlier in the day with an elderly gentleman named Ralph Farnum. The 104-year-old Farnum was one of the few living veterans of the Revolutionary War and had witnessed the British army's defeat and surrender at Saratoga, New York.

Arrangements were made for him to have a private audience with the prince at the nearby Revere House. Farnum was now nearly deaf and in poor health, but the significance of the moment was not lost on him. He had fought for American independence from King George III, and now was sitting down with his great-great grandson, a man who would be king someday himself.

"I hear so much in praise of the Prince of Wales that I fear the people will all turn Royalists," Farnum quipped, to the amusement of his royal host.[40] He explained that he wished to pay his respects to the British royal family to show that "past animosities were forgotten."[41]

The veteran was asked about his recollections of General John Burgoyne's surrender in 1777. Farnum was complimentary and called Burgoyne "a brave officer" who was facing dwindling supply lines and "wretched" conditions.[42]

"But you got the best of him there," answered one member of the prince's royal party. The brief conversation lasted about fifteen minutes and when it was over Prince Albert Edward signed an autograph for Farnum and the two men shook hands warmly.

The prince and his entourage soon left Boston and concluded their North American tour with a stop in Maine where they boarded the Royal Navy's HMS Hero for a return sail to the United Kingdom. On November 15, 1860, the young Prince of Wales arrived home—fittingly—in Plymouth, England.

GOVERNOR ANDREW AND THE RETURN OF THE COLORS (1865)

You must, however, pardon us if we give them up with profound regret.

DECEMBER 22, 1865: An emotional Governor John Albion Andrew stood atop the State House steps and watched as the soldiers arrived carrying the remnants of their regimental colors. Their battered battle flags were not the only visible Civil War scars.

At the front of the procession was Sergeant Thomas Plunkett, a double-amputee who lost his limbs during the Battle of Fredericksburg. When his unit's flag bearer was killed, Plunkett tossed away his own rifle and heroically picked up the colors to protect the honor of his regiment and guide his fellow troops—until he was struck by an artillery shell that severed his right arm and left hand. Yet Plunkett still managed to clasp the blood-soaked flag to his chest long enough for relief to come.

Governor Andrew.
Library of Congress.

Now, shortly after one o'clock on a sunny but stingingly cold December day, Sergeant Plunkett was leading a flag procession of a different sort. Nearly two thousand returning Civil War soldiers from fifty different regiments had turned out for a ceremonial march through the snow-covered streets of Boston, surrounded by vast crowds of adoring spectators.

The parade ended on Beacon Street in front of the State House and the flag bearers from each regiment arranged themselves in order on the capitol steps. The upstairs balcony was filled with women waving colorful handkerchiefs in the air while a patriotic band played in the background. Ceremonial cannon fire blasted from the Boston Common and seemingly shook the State House dome itself.

The distinctive battle flags of each regiment were originally issued by Governor Andrew four years earlier as the volunteer soldiers first headed off to war. After the formal end of hostilities, the United States War Department ordered that the regimental colors be retired and returned to their home states. Governor Andrew had selected this day, December 22, for the ceremony given its symbolic importance as Forefathers' Day, the anniversary of the Pilgrims landing in Plymouth.

Artist Edward Simmons' mural depicting the return of the colors was unveiled in 1902. Governor Andrew is shown on the State House steps receiving the battle flags. *Author image.*

Surrounded by state leaders and other dignitaries, the governor descended several steps and greeted Major General Darius Couch, who would formally present the returning colors on behalf of the several dozen flag bearers arrayed in front of the State House. After an opening prayer, General Couch stepped forward to address the governor. A cheer went forth and the troops lifted up their tattered colors.

"We have come here today as the representatives of the army of volunteers furnished by Massachusetts for the suppression of the rebellion, bringing these colors in order to return them to the state who entrusted them to our keeping," Couch declared.[43]

"You must, however, pardon us if we give them up with profound regret––for these tattered shreds … attest the sacrifices that have been made, the courage and constancy shown, that the nation might live," he said.[44]

Governor Andrew stared out at the sea of battle flags, including one from the all-Black 54th Massachusetts regiment that he had helped organize, and was clearly touched by the pageantry. He had declined to run for re-election and was due to leave office in two weeks, so this would be one of his final acts in office.[45]

In his remarks, which were later reprinted and widely distributed, he praised the heroic regiments returning after four years of civil war and welcomed their banners back to the Commonwealth.

"Proud memories of many a field; sweet memories alike of valor and friendship; sad memories of fraternal strife; tender memories of our fallen brothers and sons, whose dying eyes looked last upon their flaming folds; grand memories of heroic virtues, sublimed by grief; exultant memories of the great and final victory of our country, our Union, and the righteous cause; thankful memories of a deliverance wrought out for human nature itself, unexampled by any former achievements of arms; immortal memories with immortal honors blended, twine around these splintered staffs, weave themselves along the warp and woof of these familiar flags, war-worn, begrimmed and baptized with blood."[46]

The governor received rousing applause after his remarks. After the brief ceremony the flag bearers marched up the front steps and through the front doors into the State House where the returning colors were deposited in Doric Hall.

The touching scene was later depicted by artist Edward Simmons in a mural painted on the east wall of a new State House annex. The grand circular hall, featuring Italian marble and a large stained-glass window, was built to house the flags and serve as a permanent tribute to Civil War soldiers. Today the space is better known as Memorial Hall.[47]

Chapter 9

PIONEERING LAWMAKERS SWORN IN (1867)

*These men are chosen, not as a joke or satire, but in
honest earnest, because they are fit for the position,
and because they have rights which white men
at last respect.*

JANUARY 2, 1867: Among the one-hundred-and-fifty-plus new state legislators taking the oath of office for the January term, two new members stood out: Edwin Garrison Walker of Charlestown and Charles Lewis Mitchell of Boston. [48] Walker and Mitchell were the first Black representatives ever elected in Massachusetts and among the first in the nation.

Walker, a leathermaker and newly-minted attorney, was elected from a predominately white and Irish district in Charlestown. Mitchell, a printer by trade who lost his right foot serving in the Civil War, was elected from Boston's wealthy Ward Six, which included a sizable Black population.

The new legislative session was gaveled to order in the House chamber shortly after eleven o'clock on a cold Wednesday morning. It had snowed four to five inches earlier in the week and the snow was still melting on the streets below. After an opening prayer the two men, along with their fellow

Charles L. Mitchell of Boston (left) and Edwin G. Walker of Charlestown (right) were the first two Black legislators elected in Massachusetts. Walker, often known by his nickname "Judge," continued his legal career after his term ended and later served as president of the Colored National League and the Equal Rights Association. After his service, Mitchell was appointed as a customs inspector, a position he held until his retirement in 1909. *Wethersfield Historical Society* and *New York Public Library.*

representatives, took the oath of office from Governor Alexander Hamilton Bullock.

Following customary practice, the House speaker selected various members to carry out ceremonial functions during the inauguration and Walker was one of five members selected to carry out elections for the clerk. Mitchell was appointed to the standing Committee on Printing and Walker to the Committee on Federal Relations.

The pair were assigned seats in the chamber mixed among their fellow representatives: Walker in the rear of the Third Division sitting next to another Charlestown legislator, and Mitchell in the middle of the Fourth Division, between a pair of South Shore legislators.[49] Like nearly all of the 241 House members, the men were members of the Republican Party, though Walker was reportedly nominated with the help of Democrats and later changed his party affiliation.

By most accounts Walker and Mitchell appeared to be warmly welcomed by the majority of their colleagues and the press. "These men are chosen, not as a joke or satire, but in honest earnest, because they are fit for the position, and because they have rights which white men at last respect," wrote a Springfield newspaper, where Mitchell once worked as a printer.[50]

"We cheerfully chronicle the election of two colored men to the Massachusetts legislature," another paper wrote. "Both are said to be men that will ably and faithfully execute the trust assigned them."

The Salem Register also praised the pair, calling Walker a "well-known and highly respected member of the … bar," and Mitchell a "modest, intelligent, brave-hearted man." The newspaper also noted the pioneering aspect of their history-making election. "We regard this election … as doubly valuable, because they will pave the way for a further recognition of the colored man's place in office," it wrote.

Walker and Mitchell also shared a connection through William Lloyd Garrison, publisher of the *Liberator* newspaper, which, with the Civil War over, had recently ended its lengthy publication run. Mitchell worked as a pressman at the *Liberator* before enlisting in the 54th infantry regiment, and Walker, the son of famed abolitionist David Walker, was given his middle name in honor of Garrison.

Wendell Phillips, another prominent abolitionist connected to Garrison, beamed with pride upon learning that Walker and Mitchell would "take their place under the dome of the State House."[51] He interrupted a scheduled lecture in Boston on election night to share the news with his audience. After offering warm praise for both men, Phillips invoked the spirit of Walker's late father, calling his son "a fitting representative of the aggressive, indomitable, fearless spirit which cast the first spear of defiance into the hosts of slavery even years before the *Liberator* spread its banner to the breeze."[52]

That same evening over in Mitchell's West End neighborhood a crowd of Black residents marched in the streets with drums and songs to rejoice at the news of his election. A group assembled in Mitchell's front yard, and he opened his window to welcome and address the joyful gathering. He also offered greetings to his fellow representative-elect in Charlestown, where he said voters had "elected within the shadow of Bunker Hill, not one of [Confederate General Robert] Toombs' slaves, but a free and enlightened colored citizen."[53]

Following their inauguration both men got to work in their new roles. Mitchell introduced his first piece of legislation later in January, a bill to incorporate the West Boston Savings Bank, while Walker filed a local bill relative to a wharf on the Mystic River and also gave his "maiden" speech on the topic.

Both legislators supported resolutions opposing the adoption of the Fourteenth Amendment to the United States Constitution, which was up for ratification in Massachusetts. The men were not alone in their opposition. A majority of Walker's Committee on Federal Relations also recommended

John James Smith, a prominent Beacon Hill barber, was the first Black legislator in Massachusetts to serve more than one term. Smith later served on the Boston Common Council and was active in several fraternal organizations, including the Masons. *State House Library.*

against adoption, arguing that the amendment did not sufficiently protect civil rights or ensure Black suffrage. Wendell Phillips called it "a swindle."

During the final floor debate in the House, Walker himself stood and gave an impassioned speech on the matter. "We are bound to pause before we give our assent to a measure that carries with it into the Constitution of the United States, not the old institution of slavery, but a system of serfdom equally as disgraceful to the American people," he said.

The Fourteenth Amendment was ultimately ratified by the Massachusetts House by a comfortable margin, but twenty-seven other representatives joined Walker and Mitchell in voting against it. The men may have lost that vote, but their concerns were ultimately heeded—in part, at least—with the ratification of the Fifteenth Amendment granting Black male suffrage some two years later.

Walker and Mitchell were no longer in the legislature, however, to approve that measure. Neither man was re-elected at the end of their one-year term. That November the most spirited debate in Massachusetts was not over race—or civil rights—but rather … spirits. Party tickets were split among factions advocating for a prohibition on alcohol and those who only favored licensing it.

In his Charlestown ward, Walker competed in a crowded six-man field for two available seats but was edged out by a Democrat and another man running on the pro-licensing platform. In Boston's Ward Six, there was similar confusion at party caucuses with as many as five different tickets handed out on election day. A sizable Black vote turned out once again, but Mitchell was not renominated on all of the Republican tickets and another Black man was elected instead, John James Smith, a Beacon Hill barber and active abolitionist.[54]

Smith was re-elected for a second term in the House the following year and eventually served three terms in total. Several other Black legislators were elected over the next decade, including George Lewis Ruffin, Lewis Hayden and Joshua Bowen Smith.

The early gains in Black representation did not continue. In the first half century after the Civil War fourteen different Black legislators served in the Massachusetts House of Representatives. Over the next fifty years there would be just seven.[55]

Chapter 10

A MASHPEE FARMER
MAKES HISTORY (1886)

*My people are as poor as any on the whole Cape,
and they ought to have the same law as
Dennis, Harwich and Yarmouth.*

JANUARY 13, 1886: When Representative Watson F. Hammond raised his hand to take the oath of office and start the new session, it marked another first. The forty-eight-year-old Mashpee Republican was the first known Native American legislator in the history of the Massachusetts General Court.

Hammond had defeated Barnstable Democrat Abel D. Makepeace, a prominent cranberry grower, by seventy-seven votes in November to win the Second Barnstable district seat. His election was no fluke. Described as "a man of strict integrity and business principle,"[56] Hammond was an active Mashpee resident who had served as town moderator, surveyor, school board member, selectman and church deacon. He managed to win the seat despite the fact that his hometown of Mashpee had only 347 total voters.[57]

Hammond had lost his father at a young age and spent most of his younger years at sea, including on a whaling ship out of New Bedford. He was an accomplished farmer and had invented a machine used for sifting cranberries that was later granted a U.S. patent.[58] He was a descendant of the Montauk, and his wife was the daughter of a well-known Wampanoag religious leader known as Reverend "Blind" Joe Amos.

The history-making nature of Hammond's election did not go unnoted, even outside of the state. A telegraph wire brief referring to him as the first "North American Indian" ever elected to the Massachusetts General Court was picked up by a number of out-of-state newspapers, including in New Jersey, Connecticut, and Pennsylvania. There was also much pride within the Mashpee Wampanoag community to see one of their own elevated to a position of leadership in the state. Sharing the sentiment of many following his election, one friend wrote of Hammond: "The rightful claimant of America; may his services ... be as meritorious as was the original claim to the soil."[59]

Rep. Watson F. Hammond is the first known Native American legislator to serve in the Massachusetts legislature. *National Museum of the American Indian Archives Center, Smithsonian Institution.*

After his swearing in, the new legislator took his seat on the right side of the House chamber, sitting between a blacksmith from Southboro and a bookseller from Boston—both Republicans, like the majority of the 240-member body. Hammond was appointed to serve on the Roads and Bridges Committee.[60]

Later that month, Hammond filed his first bill, a petition regulating the use of net fishing in Vineyard Sound. He hoped to prevent large seining boats from overfishing the waters between his district and Martha's Vineyard, which served as a natural spawning ground for bluefish. The bill was advanced by the Fisheries and Game Committee and came up for a vote in May, giving him an opportunity to make his history-making inaugural speech.

HOUSE OF REPRESENTATIVES.

J. Q. A. BRACKETT, Speaker.

Districts.	Representatives.	Residence.	Date of Birth.	Native Place.	Occupation.	1st Year in Leg.
Barnstable County.						
No. 1,	Chas. Dillingham,	Sandwich,	Sept. 27, 1821,	Sandwich,	Farmer, Supt. Sch'ls,	1861.[1]
2,	Watson F. Hammond,	Mashpee,	May 24, 1837,	Mashpee,	Farmer,	1886.
3,	Geo. H. Loring,	Yarmouth,	July 26, 1834,	Yarmouth,	Retired,	1886.
4,	Ambrose N Doane,	Harwich,	Nov. 22, 1839,	Harwich,	Wholes'e Fish Deal'r,	1885.
5,	Isaiah C. Young,	Wellfleet,	Sept. 29, 1846,	Wellfleet,	Merchant,	1886.
6,	Benjamin D. Atkins,	Provincetown,	July 20, 1832,	Provincetown,	Mechanic,	1885.
Berkshire County.						
No. 1,	Benj. Franklin Mills,	Williamstown,	Mar. 13, 1816,	Williamstown,	Farmer,	1856.[1]
2,	George H. Kearn,	North Adams,	Jan. 6, 1839,	Bridgep't, Conn.,	Manufacturer,	1886.
	Alexander W. Fulton,	North Adams,	April 30, 1842,	Born at sea,	Shoemaker,	1886.
3,	John C. Crosby,	Pittsfield,	June 15, 1859,	Sheffield, Mass.,	Lawyer,	1886.
	Lorenzo H. Gamwell,	Pittsfield,	April –, 1821,	Tyringham,	Lawyer,	1886.
4,	Frank E. Mason,	Savoy,	July 25, 1859,	Savoy,	Farmer,	1886.
5,	Samuel H. Norton,	Otis,	Oct. 17, 1831,	Otis,	Merchant,	1886.
6,	Charles H. Dorr,	Richmond,	Jan. 7, 1847,	Florida, N Y.,	Farmer,	1886.
7,	Charles J Burget,	Gt. Barrington	May 22, 1837,	Alford, Mass.,	Merchant,	1886.
8,	Edward D. Andrus,	Sheffield,	July 5, 1838,	Sheffield,	Farmer,	1886.

[1] Senate.

Representative Hammond is listed in the House Journal with his fellow Barnstable County legislators. *State House Library.*

"My people are as poor as any on the whole Cape, and they ought to have the same law as Dennis, Harwich and Yarmouth," Hammond said in his first formal remarks from the House floor on May 3, 1886. "The big boats with nets must be made to use deep water and leave the rest for hook and line."[61]

Hammond earned some nodding approval for his remarks. "His speech was not as elevated as a harangue of [noted Native American orators] Logan or Pontiac, but it was as good as half of the members of the House could make," one newspaper declared.[62]

His bill was amended and then passed by the full House. During the remainder of his one-year term, Hammond also filed legislation to allow separate ballots for school committee elections and co-sponsored a bill to establish Arbor Day in Massachusetts.

Despite some initial successes as a new legislator, Hammond was not re-elected for a second term. A realignment of legislative districts into a broader Cape Cod region shifted power away from the smaller Mashpee, and when it came time for Republican delegates to select their nominees later that fall, he was edged out by candidates from Sandwich and Yarmouth. Hammond, and another unsuccessful Republican candidate from Bourne, tried to split off and run on a ticket as Independent Republicans, but neither was successful.

Following his service in the legislature, Hammond remained civically, religiously, and politically active in Mashpee for many years. He and his wife celebrated their golden wedding anniversary in 1910, and he later died in 1916, at the age of 82.

Chapter 11

YOUNG HELEN KELLER SHARES A VISION FOR CHANGE (1903)

*Their education was a delight, and a privilege,
but for what have they been educated?*

MARCH 6, 1903: The speakers at the State House hearing included a prominent doctor, a respected judge and a former congressman, but the most memorable testimony came from a twenty-two-year-old college student who could neither see nor hear the proceedings.

Helen Keller had lost her sight and hearing as an infant and relied on a trusted companion to help communicate. Yet none of those obstacles seemingly held her back and she had already blazed a remarkable academic career.

Her intellectual prowess was on display as early as eight years old when local newspapers raved about her mastery of mathematics and geometry. The story of the brilliant young deaf and blind girl soon captured national attention and Keller began studying at the Perkins School for the Blind in Boston. Now the

Helen Keller in 1905.
Library of Congress.

At the time of her testimony before the legislature, Helen Keller was a student at Radcliffe College. She graduated cum laude the following year with a Bachelor of Arts degree. *Perkins School for the Blind.*

Cambridge resident was about to graduate from Radcliffe College and publish her first book, an autobiography.

When the legislature's Committee on Education scheduled a hearing on a bill for a new commission to investigate services for the adult blind in March of 1903, Keller was naturally invited to attend. Her presence drew a large audience to the State House hearing room.[63]

Keller was joined by her teacher and friend Anne Sullivan, who had worked with her since she was a young girl. During the hearing Sullivan repeated Keller's testimony to ensure that her words were understood, though observers said they were able to understand if they sat nearby.

Keller used the opportunity to advocate for vocational training services for the adult blind. She felt strongly that education was just one part of the equation and the blind needed employment skills and opportunity in order to be more self-sufficient.

"It has long been my earnest desire that something be done to help the blind support themselves. It is terrible to be blind and to be uneducated; but it is worse for the blind who have finished their education to be idle. Their very education becomes a burden because they cannot use it," she explained.[64]

A state training facility would help the blind develop these skills and put their education to better use, she told the committee in urging support for the bill.

"I remember the distress of many blind people I have known, who, after finishing their education, could find no means of supporting themselves, because no one helped them to find positions in which they could turn what

Keller met nearly every United State President to hold office in her lifetime, including a pair from Massachusetts—Calvin Coolidge in 1926, and John F. Kennedy (above) in 1961. *Perkins School for the Blind.*

they have been taught to practical use. The greater their ambition to do useful work, the more cruel their disappointment," Keller said.

"They think, think, think in the long days that are nights. They have been taught to aspire; they have read books; perhaps they have tasted the 'higher education,' and now they are sent back from school, and often to poor homes, with nothing to do, except to contrast with bitter longing the school days, full of books, and music, with the helpless, inactive present. Their education was a delight, and a privilege, but for what have they been educated?" she asked.

Establishing a commission would accomplish three things, she told the legislators. It would allow the blind to better support themselves, reduce the state's burden of caring for them, and set an example for other states. The commonwealth had already waited too long to act and now it needed to lead, she pleaded.

"It is not higher education that the blind need, it is not Greek and Latin, but an industrial training and some one with influence and authority to help them to a place in the industrial world," she said.

Keller was one of the final speakers at the morning hearing and she received hearty applause following her testimony. The event was widely covered in the press, which called her address eloquent, moving, and compelling.[65]

Even after the hearing, Keller and others continued to advocate for training services for the blind. Their lobbying paid off. In August, Governor John Bates appointed a commission to investigate the condition of the adult blind and report back to the legislature with recommendations.

President Coolidge and Helen Keller in 1926. *Library of Congress.*

Their work eventually led to the creation of a permanent state agency to be known as the Massachusetts Commission for the Blind, which was tasked, in part, with improving employment opportunities for adults who were blind. Keller was named one of the original five commissioners.[66]

Chapter 12

ROOSEVELT TAKES ON HIS PROTÉGÉ (1912)

The fight is on and I am stripped to the buff.

FEBRUARY 26, 1912: Former President Theodore Roosevelt was attending a women's luncheon at the fashionable Chilton Club in Boston's Back Bay when the invitation arrived. It was a cold Monday afternoon in February and the former president had already caused quite a stir, even before his arrival in Boston two days earlier.

Roosevelt had been making noises about seeking a third term in the White House by challenging his former protégé, current President William Howard Taft. Following a speech in Ohio the week prior, Roosevelt made his intentions clear. "My hat is in the ring," he said. "The fight is on and I am stripped to the buff."

Roosevelt felt that his successor had strayed from his progressive principles and launched an ambitious campaign to defeat Taft and recapture the Republican nomination. After a stop in New York, Roosevelt arrived in Boston via train and planned a packed agenda, including a series of meetings with political allies and government leaders; a speech to a Massachusetts Progressive Republicans group; and a Harvard-Yale hockey game.

The new invitation came from members of the Massachusetts legislature during his women's luncheon. It was a hastily organized effort by pro-Roosevelt lawmakers to have him address the body. The former president readily agreed to attend later that afternoon. "Are you sure that will give you time enough?" he was asked. Roosevelt smiled and nodded affirmatively.[67]

The order to formally invite the former president was quickly introduced by a Cambridge representative and broadly agreed upon in the Massachusetts House, though not all legislators were enthusiastic. The Roosevelt-Taft split had already caused deep fissures in the party.

Roosevelt left the Chilton Club by open automobile and arrived under the State House arch shortly before three o'clock with a press contingent in tow. He dropped his top coat at a nearby office and then proceeded to the House Chamber, where he was escorted by the sergeant at arms, who wore a traditional silk hat and cockade and held a ceremonial mace.[68]

House members stood and applauded as the center doors of the chamber swung open and Roosevelt marched down the aisle toward the desk of House Speaker Grafton Cushing. Cushing was an old friend and fellow Harvard graduate, though he was leery of Roosevelt's recent calls for judicial recall

"My hat is in the ring," Roosevelt declared shortly before arriving in Boston, where he gave a key speech at the State House. *Boston Public Library Leslie Jones Collection.*

and popular referendum policies. Many of the Republican House members felt a similar conflict and the reception for the former president was polite, but muted.

"We have with us a very distinguished American who represents the very best and highest in our national life," Cushing said in his brief introduction, which some observers later called perfunctory.

Roosevelt stood behind the speaker's mahogany desk and bowed solemnly to his audience before commencing his speech. He held some notes in his right hand and clenched his left in a fist which he occasionally used to pound on the table for emphasis. His demeanor was described as serious and determined.

"It is a great honor which I deeply appreciate to be permitted to address this legislative body composed of the representatives of that great and historic Commonwealth which has ever stood foremost in the unending battle for liberty and right secured within the law."[69] Roosevelt said to begin his remarks. His attempts at flattery had mixed effect with the audience in the chamber, which was nonetheless filled with spectators eager to hear what the ex-president had to say.

Roosevelt knew that a recent speech given in Ohio had ruffled some feathers, even among some of his former Republican supporters, and he wanted to use this occasion to clarify his views on the issue of judicial reform. He was not advocating for the popular recall of judges, as some claimed, or perhaps misconstrued, but rather the recall of judicial decisions.

"My position is, if the people know enough to make the constitution, they know enough in the last resort to interpret it," he said. "I am not advocating the recall of the judge. I am advocating the recall of legalism to justice."

Roosevelt made clear his plan applied only to legislative acts deemed unconstitutional by the courts. If the legislature and the governor had signed off on a law which was later rejected by the courts then he felt the people deserved an opportunity to pass final judgement. Critics who claimed this would subject judicial decision-making to popular whims failed to appreciate the lengthy timeline involved, which would afford ample time for rational reflection, he said.

He drew comparisons to the legal systems in Canada, Great Britain, and much of Europe which he said did not afford the courts power to declare a legislative act unconstitutional. Roosevelt made it clear he did not wish to go quite that far, however.

"I think that it is better that we should give the courts equal power with the legislature, but I want to keep the people as the judge between them when they differ as to whether a given law is within the power and the right of the people to pass," he explained.

Roosevelt was careful not to single out President Taft by name but he nonetheless criticized those who felt the Constitution was meant to serve a shield to guard against the passions of the people. That ran counter to what a democracy was supposed to be, he said. "If you don't believe in the people, say so, and abandon your system of government. But above all things, don't claim that you trust the people and underhandedly try to trick them out of the right of self-government," he told the audience.

By way of example, Roosevelt brought up a court case in his home state of New

Roosevelt's decision to challenge President Taft caused deep divisions within the Republican Party, which were evident during his Boston trip. In addition to the State House, he visited his alma mater Harvard University, as shown here. *Boston Public Library Leslie Jones Collection.*

York dealing with a new workers compensation law. The New York Court of Appeals had ruled one way and the U.S. Supreme Court had taken a contrary view. Roosevelt believed the people should have a chance to weigh in.

"All I ask is that the people themselves in such a case be given a chance to declare whether they will stand by the Supreme Court of the nation when it stands for human rights or by the chief court of their own state when it stands against human rights," he said and pounded his fist on the desk. "If that be revolution, make the most of it," he added, paraphrasing the words of Patrick Henry.

The speech was interrupted several times by applause, though some reports attributed the bulk of cheering to the Democrats, who were pleased to see the rival Republican party divisions. Roosevelt referred to his notes several times, but mostly spoke off the cuff in what one newspaper described as his "well-known staccato way."[70]

He also used his address to express his support for direct state and presidential primaries, rather than the traditional caucus and convention system that still dominated most states. The legislature was currently reviewing legislation to do so in Massachusetts. The reforms fit with

Roosevelt's progressive principles and his own self-interest as an insurgent presidential candidate.

The crowd applauded as Roosevelt concluded his speech, which lasted about forty minutes. He spent a few moments shaking hands and then was escorted out of the House chamber and over to the Senate where he made much briefer remarks.

Roosevelt's reception in the Senate was also cordial, though hardly enthusiastic. He largely skipped over any policy discussion and wrapped up after just a few minutes. A warmer welcome was found in the Senate lobby after the speech when Roosevelt ran into a friend with his two young boys who were eager to shake hands with the former president.

In spite of the mixed reaction, Roosevelt was pleased with his speeches and felt he had done a better job articulating his views and policy differences with Taft. "Perhaps what I said at Columbus [Ohio] will be a little clearer now," he told one friend. [71] His supporters agreed and offered hearty congratulations.

After taking some questions from the press and greeting friends, colleagues and staff, Roosevelt left the State House. He was driven to a friend's house to retrieve his belongings and then over to the Boston home of his friend Grafton Cushing, where he was to be the speaker's overnight guest.

The pair had been friends for many years and Cushing had been a strong supporter of Roosevelt's prior presidential campaigns. But if Roosevelt had assumed his speech to the Massachusetts legislature would be enough to sway skittish Republicans, he would soon be disabused of the notion. Despite their lengthy friendship, Speaker Cushing made clear he was still a Taft man.

In the race for the White House, Roosevelt realized he still had much more work to do.

Chapter 13

TAFT STRIKES BACK (1912)

Well, that's a good Irish greeting!

MARCH 18, 1912: President William Howard Taft had skipped church on Sunday and instead huddled in his study all day to work on his speech, taking only a break for lunch. In the afternoon he invited members of his cabinet to go over his remarks until it was time for him to leave the White House to catch the 5:35 p.m. train from Washington D.C. to Boston.[72]

Taft had a packed sixteen-hour day planned in Boston, including numerous speaking engagements, multiple luncheons and dinners, and a Saint Patrick's Day parade. He would also give an address before a joint session of the Massachusetts legislature, and he knew there was much riding on it. Just a few weeks earlier his friend—now rival—Theodore Roosevelt had addressed the body and Taft was eager to rebut what he felt were some unfair claims about his political views.

Roosevelt's decision to challenge him for the Republican nomination had deeply wounded him. Taft had aspirations of serving on the U.S. Supreme Court and never really wanted to be president in the first place. He'd been a member of Roosevelt's cabinet and had to be convinced to run for president in 1908 after Roosevelt made a (now regretted) pledge not to seek a third term.

Since news of the Roosevelt challenge broke, Taft had grown despondent and put on even more weight. Taft already struggled with his health and the new stress and added pounds exacerbated his sleeping woes. He compared the split with his former mentor to "a devoted friendship going to pieces like a rope of sand."[73]

Taft arrived in Boston on the Federal Express sleeping train at seven o'clock on a cloudy Monday morning. Temperatures were climbing and expected to hit sixty degrees by lunchtime. A large crowd appeared at South Station to greet the president and police had to cordon off the platform. The welcoming crew included leaders of Boston's Charitable Irish Society who led the enthusiastic crowd in a hearty three cheers for the arriving president.

"Well, that's a good Irish greeting!" Taft replied as he emerged from the station.

After coffee and rolls and a speech at the City Club, Taft was scheduled for a formal breakfast event with Mayor John Fitzgerald and city officials, where he enjoyed fried hominy and Vermont maple syrup. He was joined by his son Robert who was a student at Harvard Law School. The Tafts were hardly strangers to Massachusetts as the family had a summer home north of Boston in the town of Beverly.

Despite his political worries, Taft was his jovial self throughout the morning and felt buoyed by the words of praise he received. As he left one event, he traded light-hearted words with the mayor. "Fitzy, I see you have a new hat," he joked.

Later that morning a delegation from the State House met Taft at his hotel suite to formally extend the invitation to address the legislature. In contrast to the visit from former President Roosevelt the previous month, this invitation had been planned well ahead of time and was highly anticipated.

President Taft liked to leave Washington D.C. and spend the warmer months of the year in New England, including at his home in Beverly, Massachusetts, sometimes known as the Summer White House. *Library of Congress.*

President Taft was driven to the State House around half past noon. A crowd of cheering spectators stretched along the sidewalk outside the building and surrounded the automobile as he arrived. The crowd was "very democratic," one newspaper observed. "Men smoked their noonday pipes and groups of children from the tenements played marbles at the feet of ladies in purple and fine linen."[74]

As Taft exited the vehicle, he bowed to the left and right to acknowledge his supporters and then headed to the archway entrance. Inside, the halls were lined with more spectators and onlookers eager to see the president, who was described as "tired but happy."[75]

Before heading to the House chamber Taft paid a visit to the office of Governor Foss for an informal reception with a handful of prominent officials. This was in contrast to former President Roosevelt who had conspicuously not called on the governor during his State House visit in February. Governor Foss wore a large green Saint Patrick's Day carnation and Taft had a boutonniere of fresh violets pinned to his lapel that he'd been given at the earlier breakfast event.

After a short visit Taft and the governor were escorted to the House chamber by the sergeant at arms with the mayor, lieutenant governor and other state officials in tow. The audience rose and applauded loudly for several minutes as the contingent entered and Senate President Levi Greenwood, presiding over the joint session of the House and Senate, tried in vain several times to quiet the overflowing chamber, which was described as "a packed mass of humanity."[76]

Once the crowd had settled Greenwood banged his gavel and called the joint session to order. "The office which I hold can bring me no greater honor than introducing you to the President of the United States," he said in his short introduction.

Taft stood at the rostrum and waited as another round of applause enveloped the chamber. He reached into his cutaway coat pocket and pulled out the speech he'd worked on the day before at the White House. Taft was known as a genial and warm-hearted figure, but he disliked public speaking and his oratorical style was more ponderous and reflective, in contrast to his predecessor who came across as forceful and deliberate. Roosevelt had referred to his notes only occasionally, but Taft preferred to read his speech directly from the prepared text.

He began his address with a nod to the role that Massachusetts had played in the country's history since colonial times and then launched into a civics lesson on the role of private property rights in advancing the nation's prosperity. He warned that some aimed to curtail those rights.

"There are those who by a radical change in our institutions would force equality of condition as well as of opportunity," he said.[77]

Taft addressed the new presidential primary law which the Massachusetts legislature had just recently approved. Such direct election reforms were more likely to help his rivals, but Taft had little choice now that the law was enacted and he offered his qualified praise for the measure. So long as proper safeguards existed to ensure that only eligible voters of each party participated, he said he welcomed the change.

"Wherever full and fair notice of the election can be given, wherever adequate election safeguards can be thrown around to protect a preferential primary for the presidency, wherever the constitution of the state permits its being made applicable to the present election, I favor it and welcome it," he said.

Speaking more broadly, Taft took aim at critics who claimed he did not believe in the principles of popular government. Such talk did not reflect the reality of his administration, nor the history of the nation, he said. Chiding calls from Roosevelt and his supporters to "let the people rule" were just empty political slogans intended merely "to flatter the people," he said.

"I do not hesitate to say that the history of the last 135 years shows that the people have ruled. They may have been defeated at times by corrupt and corrupting influences. Congresses and legislatures may have halted by subterranean methods in carrying out the people's desire but, in the end, under our present Constitution and our present laws, we have had a really popular government," he said.

Taft took more direct aim at Roosevelt when he spoke about the issue of judicial recall. The former president's calls for reform were really just an attack on the judicial system itself, he argued.

"This is a government of law, not of changing economic and political theories of judicial or executive officers when those theories are in conflict with the express letter of the law. Suggestions of that sort are dangerous because they put the ship of state on a sea of troubles without a rudder.

"The strength of the government and the strength of the judiciary must rest ultimately on the confidence of the people in their integrity. Irresponsible assaults upon either in intemperate language, or on baseless assumptions of corruption or bias or incompetency, made by those whose statements have influence with any part of the people, are a serious menace to enduring government," he said.

Taft's address lasted about twenty-five minutes. The crowd reacted strongly and interrupted with a standing ovation on several occasions. His repudiation of Roosevelt "nearly raised the roof and almost startled the Sacred Codfish from his perch," one Boston newspaper colorfully declared.[78]

Taft was delighted by the strong reception to his speech. He had a dozen public events scheduled over the course of the day, but he knew this speech would get the most press coverage. It could not have gone any better, he felt. He had directly answered the Roosevelt challenge and recast the race on his own terms. If the reception he had received in Massachusetts was any barometer, he would easily recapture the nomination.[79]

Taft left the dais and made his way up the center aisle of the House chamber smiling broadly and shaking hands with cheering lawmakers. He was escorted back to the governor's office with throngs of well-wishers and supporters still clogging the corridors. As the newly energized president retrieved his top hat and prepared to exit the State House his thoughts returned to more pragmatic matters.

"Where do we go now? I'm hungry and I want something to eat," he asked.

During his visit President Taft made a campaign stop in Quincy where he attempted to rebut charges levelled against him by former President Roosevelt, once his friend and mentor. The intra-party dispute split the Republicans and Roosevelt ultimately ran for president under a third-party banner as a "Bull Moose" progressive. Both men went on to lose to Democrat Woodrow Wilson in the fall election. *Boston Public Library.*

Chapter 14

THE FAITH OF CALVIN COOLIDGE (1914)

*The Commonwealth is one. We are all members of
one body. The welfare of the weakest and the welfare
of the most powerful are inseparably bound together.*

JANUARY 7, 1914: The brief address, delivered without "fuss or feathers," was intended to lay out his principles as the new president of the state senate, but Calvin Coolidge could not have foreseen that his words would also set him on a course to the White House.

It was near lunchtime on a mild winter day in January of 1914 when forty-one-year-old Coolidge rose from the rostrum in the Senate chamber to address his colleagues. He had carefully prepared the inaugural remarks which would soon become known as his "Have Faith in Massachusetts" speech.

The gentleman from Northampton, known to "talk little but say much," had just been elected as president of the state senate by his peers. Coolidge succeeded Levi Greenwood, a Gardner Republican, who had lost his seat in the November election after being targeted by women's suffrage advocates.

Within days of Greenwood's defeat, Coolidge had deftly outmaneuvered his fellow Republican challengers and locked up enough pledges to be the next senate president in the Republican-majority chamber. "It had been a real contest, but all opposition subsided and I was unanimously nominated," he later recalled.[80]

Now, he prepared to lead the forty-member body and wanted to use his inaugural address to set the proper tone. Coolidge was dismayed by what he called a destructive "spirit of radicalism" that pervaded the political culture, including some members of his own party. "What was needed was a restoration of confidence in our institutions and in each other," he said.[81]

He knew that his new leadership role afforded him the chance to achieve a measure of influence beyond his own district and party and he was determined to capitalize on the opportunity. He drafted the speech in a plain-spoken, epigrammatic style with no wasted words, befitting his own steadfast and frugal nature. Coolidge was known as a studious, hardworking man who read the classics, often enjoyed Havana cigars, and relied on his afternoon naps.

The inaugural session was gaveled in five minutes after eleven o'clock in the morning. After the opening prayers and oaths of office, Coolidge was formally elected as the presiding officer. He rose and thanked his colleagues for the honor and then launched into his formal remarks.

"The Commonwealth is one. We are all members of one body. The welfare of the weakest and the welfare of the most powerful are inseparably bound together," he said. "Industry cannot flourish if labor languish. Transportation cannot prosper if manufactures decline. The general welfare cannot be provided for in any one act, but it is well to remember that the benefit of one is the benefit of all, and the neglect of one is the neglect of all."

Taking aim at the record number of bills that had been introduced the previous legislative term, Coolidge argued for a more conservative and restrained approach to lawmaking. "Men do not make laws. They do but discover them. Laws must be justified by something more than the will of the majority. They must rest on the eternal foundation of righteousness," he said.

He defended the role of the courts as neutral arbiters of justice and

Coolidge's "Have Faith in Massachusetts" speech helped launch his career to the Governor's office and later the White House. *Library of Congress.*

decried what he perceived as the growing politization of legal matters. Coolidge also counseled citizens not to look to government to solve all of society's ills. "Industry, thrift, character, are not conferred by act or resolve. Government cannot relieve from toil," he counseled.

In what would become the best-known sentence of his speech, the Vermont native praised his adopted home state. "Have faith in Massachusetts," Coolidge declared. "In some unimportant detail some other states may surpass her, but in the general results, there is no place on earth where the people secure, in a larger measure, the blessings of organized government, and nowhere can those functions more properly be termed self-government."

Coolidge ended his brief remarks, which clocked in fewer than one thousand words, with a call for lawmakers to stick to their convictions, stand for the common good, and have faith in the people, even in the face of opposition.

"Do the day's work. If it be to protect the rights of the weak, whoever objects, do it. If it be to help a powerful corporation better to serve the people, whatever the opposition, do that. Expect to be called a stand-patter, but don't be a stand-patter," he advised.

Governor Calvin Coolidge passes the ceremonial pewter key to his successor Governor Channing Cox. *Boston Public Library.*

Coolidge's speech had struck a more conservative tone than some of his colleagues expected from a legislator generally known for his progressive Republican views, but his remarks were nonetheless well received. The local press dutifully reprinted much of his speech and Coolidge himself was pleased by the response, which he later called "beyond my expectation."[82]

Coolidge was not above a bit of self-promotion and he sent copies of the speech to friends, family and fellow political leaders, including former President Taft and Senator Henry Cabot Lodge. Senator Lodge sent back a gracious thank you letter filled with praise for Coolidge's outspokenness in addressing "fundamental truths."

"What I like best of all is the courage with which you state those fundamental truths which it is often the fashion just now to put aside and hide. For some years past political leaders, great and small, have been talking to the people as though these truths did not exist," Lodge wrote.[83]

Coolidge proved to be a unifying choice as senate president and he was unanimously re-elected the following term. Thereafter he continued to climb the political ladder. After two terms as senate president, he ran successfully for lieutenant governor in 1915, and then governor three years later. In both cases copies of his "Have Faith in Massachusetts" speech were used as campaign materials. The speech was also reprinted from time to time in Boston area newspapers.

As governor, Coolidge garnered national attention for his response to the Boston police strike in the fall of 1919. He refused to reinstate striking officers and instead ordered out the national guard to maintain order, famously declaring: "There is no right to strike against the public safety by anybody, anywhere, any time." The rebuke cost Coolidge support with organized labor but proved popular with the general electorate and captured national press attention.

To capitalize on his new-found acclaim and showcase his rhetorical talents, Coolidge's supporters decided to repackage his existing speeches into book form for publication. The 200-page volume was entitled: "Have Faith in Massachusetts: A Collection of Speeches and Messages by Calvin Coolidge." The book contained more than thirty Coolidge speeches, but naturally featured his now famous "Have Faith in Massachusetts" remarks.

Library of Congress..

"If you like a man who has clean cut convictions and the courage to utter them with vigor and power, you will like this book. It is sound Americanism from a really great American," read one advertisement for the book, which was sold in bookstores for one dollar and fifty cents.

Newspapers across the country ran notices about Coolidge's book of speeches, further contributing to his growing national following. A second edition was rushed to the printer soon thereafter with three additional speeches, including Coolidge's remarks at the recent Republican State Convention.

In November of that year, Coolidge was easily re-elected as governor of Massachusetts, even though he was sidelined much of the campaign by the flu. His landslide victory did little to dampen growing speculation that he was bound for even higher office. Indeed, by the following summer Coolidge was formally nominated at the Republican National Convention in Chicago to serve on the Republican ticket as vice president, paired with the party's presidential nominee, Warren Harding of Ohio.

Coolidge had not been the first choice for the position among Republican party bosses who preferred a Wisconsin senator named Irvine Lenroot, but many of the rank-and-file delegates did not agree. A little-known Oregon delegate named Wallace McCamant took to the floor and, despite never having met the man, decided he would nominate Coolidge instead—after having read a copy of Have Faith in Massachusetts.

The nomination of Coolidge touched a "popular chord," McCamant recalled, and the Massachusetts governor was soundly approved by convention delegates. "I was impressed with Governor Coolidge's sterling Americanism, his fine spirit during the world war, the soundness of his thinking and the conservative trend of his thoughts," McCamant said after reading his speech.[84]

The Harding-Coolidge ticket proved a popular pairing, and the Republicans carried thirty-seven states and 404 electoral votes on route to a resounding victory in the 1920 presidential election. Coolidge's remarkable rise had brought him from the Massachusetts legislature to the vice-presidency over a six-year span. The final step occurred three years later, when President Harding died of a heart attack and Coolidge was sworn in as America's thirtieth President.

Coolidge's ascension to the White House renewed interest in his "Have Faith in Massachusetts" speech, with the public curious to learn more about the political credo of their new president. Newspapers across the country reprinted his remarks and a political biography, Have Faith in Coolidge, was promptly published.

Coolidge with his family at the White House. *Boston Public Library Leslie Jones Collection.*

Coolidge was easily re-elected to a full term of his own in 1824 and presided over a period of general prosperity for the nation. After eight years in Washington D.C., he decided he'd had enough and decided not to run for another term despite the urgings of many. True to form, the man known for his thrift and frugality issued only a terse hand-written announcement declaring his intentions: "I do not choose to run for President in 1928."

Coolidge later returned home to Northampton and devoted his remaining years to his writings, charitable endeavors, and political causes, always remaining true to the credo espoused in his famous speech to the Massachusetts legislature: "Do the day's work."

Chapter 15

THE SUFFRAGISTS AND THE PRESIDENT (1919)

No one of us will ever forget that foul bucket.

FEBRUARY 24, 1919: On the world stage, President Woodrow Wilson was earning plaudits for his peacemaking efforts after the First World War, but back home he was having less success with an increasingly defiant women's suffrage movement. The issue came to a head in front of the Massachusetts State House on a sunny winter day in 1919 when the president visited Boston.

The president's views on voting rights for women had evolved over time and he now counted himself as a committed supporter, but that did not mollify suffragists tired of waiting for change. A constitutional amendment was still muddling its way through a divided Congress and so when Wilson arrived on February 24 after returning from Europe, a group of activists from the National Women's Party seized the opportunity to apply some political pressure.[85]

The women assembled in the morning near the State House with colorful pickets, protest signs, and a large American flag. "Mr. President, how long must women wait for liberty?" read one sign. "Mr. President, what will you do for woman suffrage?" said another. One prominent suffragist from Cambridge burned a rolled-up paper purported to be a copy of President Wilson's speech on democracy.

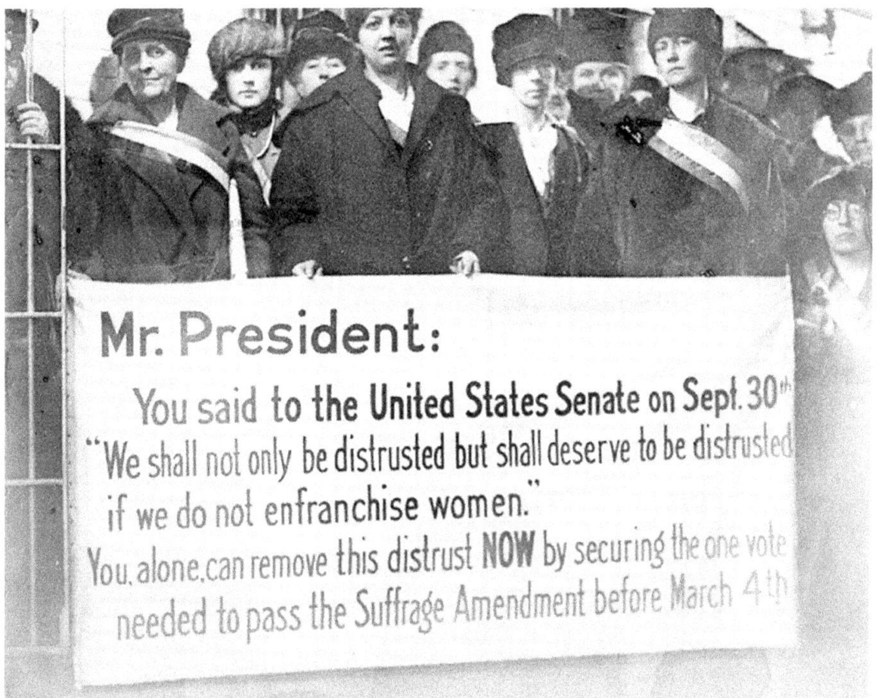

A group of women arrested at the State House later unfurled this sign in front of the Charles Street Jail calling on President Wilson to do more to pass the women's voting amendment. *Historic New England Library and Archives.*

Plans for the presidential visit included a celebratory parade past the State House where the governor and other dignitaries would be waiting to offer a triumphal greeting. The women had other plans, however, and they slipped through the crowd with their purple and gold banners and positioned themselves in front of the reviewing stand where they could block the president's view when he marched by.

Security was tight and police warned the women to disperse, but they refused. After several futile efforts to clear the scene, twenty-two women were arrested for loitering. A patrol wagon arrived at the State House and the women were escorted to the House of Detention in the lower level of the city courthouse. Most of the women spent the night locked up in jail, packed four to a cell with a pair of wide iron shelves and an open toilet for each.[86]

"It is a most extraordinary thing. Thousands loitered from curiosity on the day the President arrived. Twenty-two loitered for liberty, and only those who loitered for liberty were arrested," said Agnes Morey, a leader of the women's party.[87]

The next day a judge ordered the women to pay five-dollar fines, which most also refused, and they were taken to the Charles Street Jail to serve brief sentences. These cells were cleaner, but they lacked modern plumbing and, in lieu of a toilet, featured a heavy wooden bucket filled with water. "No one of us will ever forget that foul bucket," Morey recalled.[88]

The women were soon bailed out and their ordeal ended without further incident, but the political damage had been done. Supportive telegrams flooded in from across the nation and the Boston press splashed news of the jailed suffragettes across their front pages. The story quickly spread to newspapers from Maine to California. Some of the news coverage was mocking or demeaning, but the women also earned plenty of praise for their bravery. Regardless, the demonstration achieved its goal of applying pressure on President Wilson and congressional leaders.

Agnes Morey headed up the Massachusetts branch of the National Women's Party and helped organize the State House demonstration during President Wilson's visit.

Three months later the United State Senate finally mustered enough votes to pass a constitutional amendment affirming women's right to vote.

Chapter 16

VETERAN VISITS FOR THE AGES (1924)

*When you see any of us old fellows stumping along
this week you never have a doubt we thank God that
we were born when we did ... to get in the service
when Abraham Lincoln called.*

AUGUST 11, 1924: The State House was adorned with patriotic bunting and banners to welcome the thousands of Union veterans arriving in Boston for the 58th annual Grand Army of the Republic (G.A.R.) national convention. The fraternal organization (which later added auxiliary membership open to women) was created after the Civil War and became a powerful force advocating for veterans' causes.

Boston had hosted the national encampment, as it was known, several times and most recently in 1917. The event drew an estimated six thousand visitors to the state and featured several days of ceremonial parades, speeches, concerts, religious services, and general camaraderie.

Library of Congress.

The State House was resplendent with patriotic regalia to welcome thousands of Civil War veterans and their families attending the Grand Army of the Republic (G.A.R.) national convention in 1924. *Boston Public Library.*

The festivities included a visit to the Legion Department headquarters located inside the State House, where a number of the veterans viewed an art gallery and reminisced by singing Civil War marching songs. Afterwards they gathered on the front steps of the State House for a photo.

One group of four veterans from the Midwest who had brought their musical instruments along with them during a tour of the State House bumped into the governor's assistant in the Hall of Flags. The veterans were asked if they might play a song for the governor, and an impromptu concert soon followed in the Executive Council chambers. Playing violins and guitars, the veterans performed "Marching through Georgia" and "Swanee River" for a delighted Governor Cox who passed out cigars and thanked the men for the serenade.[89]

By now most of the veterans were at an advanced age, including Dr. R.B. Tyler visiting from Joplin, Missouri, who claimed to be one of the youngest at age seventy-two.[90] The Grand Army Parade included three centenarians from Massachusetts riding together in one automobile, while Civil War veteran drummers and fifers, most in their eighties, marched alongside. The parade route was shortened to accommodate the advanced age of most of the participants.

"When you see any of us old fellows stumping along this week you never have a doubt we thank God that we were born when we did … to get in the service when Abraham Lincoln called," said Corporal James Tanner, a past G.A.R. commander.[91]

At the time of the Boston encampment there were still 65,382 living Civil War veterans on the rolls, but their numbers were dwindling. The national encampments continued until 1949, when there were still sixteen documented living members, and the Grand Army of the Republic formally dissolved when the last surviving Civil War veteran died in 1956.[92]

A MEETING FOR THE AGES: Captain Edwin Wyer, age 90, fought in the Battle of Bull Run during the Civil War and was the state's oldest living veteran. World War I veteran Terry McCloskey, a Dorchester resident who lied about his age and enlisted in the Army at the age of 14, was the youngest. The two men met at the State House as the guest of Governor Channing Cox on February 27, 1922. *Library of Congress.*

Chapter 17

'MADAME SPEAKER' (1926)

*We who are about to subject ourselves to your
guidance do so with full confidence in your integrity,
ability and efficiency.*

FEBRUARY 18, 1926: A wave of cheers and applause erupted as seventy-six-year-old Sylvia Donaldson rose from her chair in the third division of the Massachusetts House chamber. It was a rainy Thursday afternoon in the city of Boston, and history was about to be made.

The retired schoolteacher from Brockton was hard to miss. Standing nearly six feet tall in a silk blue dress, with her white hair pulled back in a fashionable chignon and stern blue eyes staring behind a pair of dark spectacles, Donaldson was just one of only two female legislators. She gave off a stately and dignified air, and if she was in any way rattled by the attention now bestowed upon her, it did not show.

Donaldson laid down a pair of violet and rosebud bouquets she'd been given and made her way to the front of the House chamber which was teeming with spectators from the floor up to the visitor galleries. Accompanying her were Representative Victor Jewett of Lowell, a vinegar manufacturer who served as Majority Leader, and Representative Harriet Russell Hart of Lynn, a newly elected member and the only other woman serving in the state legislature.

House Speaker John Hull stood at the rostrum with his outstretched hand gripping a wooden gavel. Like Donaldson, Hull was a member of the

Republican Party, which still dominated the 240-member chamber by a nearly three-to-one margin. The Republicans also held the state senate and the governor's office, though Democrats were slowly increasing their ranks.

The extended applause continued as Donaldson approached Hull on the dais. After handing over his gavel, the speaker descended from the rostrum and took a seat on the floor with the rest of the House members. There were extra seats arrayed around the chamber to accommodate the many guests in attendance as news of the impending event had leaked out in the local newspapers several days earlier.

State Representative Sylvia Donaldson of Brockton. *Falmouth Museums on the Green.*

With their traditional roles now reversed, Donaldson stood at the rostrum wielding the speaker's gavel and called on Hull from his seat. His next words would be a first in the nearly one-hundred-and-fifty-year history of the institution:

"Madame Speaker!" Hull proclaimed.

"Yours, Madame Speaker, is a distinct and signal honor … you now stand there as the representative of all the women of this great Commonwealth of Massachusetts, and happily and signally demonstrate the fact that today neither the ballot, nor public office, nor the highest gift within the power of this House, is denied to any citizen 'on account of sex'," he continued.

"I, too, am honored on this occasion, because I have been permitted to be the first member of this ancient assembly to address the Chair as 'Madame Speaker'. I hope that my relatives, friends and acquaintances may also point with pride, in the years to come, to this fact. … Madame Speaker, we who are about to subject ourselves to your guidance do so with full confidence in your integrity, ability and efficiency. Madame Speaker, we salute you!"

Hull wrapped up his brief remarks and returned to his seat while Donaldson remained standing on the rostrum. The House clerk stood to her right in his customary position, ready to offer assistance, but she needed none. As a two-term lawmaker with decades of classroom experience, she was comfortable in her role and well-schooled in the minutia of legislative procedure. Her father, George Washington Donaldson, had also been a state legislator himself.

Donaldson was used to the extra attention that came with being one of the first-ever female members in the Massachusetts legislature. Donaldson won election in 1922 from one of two seats in the Tenth Plymouth District, a Republican stronghold in the city of Brockton. That same year Susan

Fitzgerald, a Boston Democrat, was also voted in and the pair made history as the first women elected in the state's history.

THE ARRIVAL of two female legislators to the State House in January of 1923 was heralded as "a new era in the public life of the commonwealth," coming two years after the ratification of the Nineteenth Amendment that formally gave women the right to vote.

Donaldson had retired from teaching in 1919 and was then elected to her local school committee.[93] She remained active in her community as a member of the local Red Cross, Girl Scouts, and Brockton Women's Club. She was originally from Falmouth and later moved to Brockton when it was still known as North Bridgewater.[94] In the summer of 1922, she announced

FIRST WOMEN LEGISLATORS CREATE SENSATION AT STATE CAPITOL.

Boston Globe, January 4, 1923.

her candidacy for the state legislature and later that fall earned 3,306 votes, outpacing her nearest Democratic opponent by nearly four hundred votes.

On the morning of her inauguration Donaldson had taken the 8:17 a.m. train in from Brockton. A new private lounging room for female legislators had been set up near the fourth-floor gallery so that the women would not be forced to endure the regular smoke-filled House member's lounge where the men congregated.

Throngs of newspaper photographers followed her around the building, though she did not much care for the press and initially refused to have her picture taken at all. Her colleague and fellow trailblazer, Representative Fitzgerald, was less camera shy and eagerly chatted up the coterie of staffers, journalists, and curiosity seekers who flocked around the two new arrivals.

After attending a morning caucus with her fellow Republicans, Donaldson was ushered into the office of Governor Channing Cox for a private swearing in ceremony. The governor administered the oath of office and then posed with the women on the State House balcony overlooking the Boston Common. The added pomp and circumstance delayed the women and they ended up being a few minutes late for their inaugural House session.

Donaldson had worn a stately blue hat with gray flowers and "a drooping lane of gray ostrich" along the brim for the occasion, not realizing that hats ran afoul of the House rules of decorum. She learned her lesson quickly and in the four years since had certainly earned the respect of her peers and the voters of her district. (Her colleague Rep. Fitzgerald was less fortunate and lost her bid for re-election the following term.)

AFTER THE APPLAUSE in the chamber had subsided, Donaldson gaveled the House to order and settled into her role as "Madame Speaker." While she certainly appreciated the significance of the moment, she chose not to offer any public remarks of her own but instead

DONALDSON, M. SYLVIA, 191 Newbury St., Brockton, 10th Plymouth House District, Republican.

Born: Falmouth, July 12, 1849.

Educated: Boston Univ. Normal Art.

Profession: Dist. school principal, Brockton, until 1919.

Organization: Audubon Soc., Daughters of Revolution, Nat'l Education Ass'n, League of Women Voters, Women's Civic Federation.

Public office: School Board, Mass. House 1923-'24.

State House Library.

plunged into legislative business, which on this day included handling a variety of appropriation bills, orders, committee reports, senate amendments, and roll call votes.

Unaccustomed as they were to the new title of the presiding officer, some of the representatives mistakenly addressed her as "Mr. Speaker," while others—no doubt cognizant of the added attention on the day's proceedings—went out of their way to flatter, speechify, or pontificate. One of the younger democratic members noted the "grace and charm" of the presiding officer.

The women who packed the visitor's gallery for the historic occasion cheered heartily for Donaldson, but they were not always thrilled with her political views. Earlier in the day, Donaldson had testified against legislation prioritized by the League of Women Voters and the Mass. Council of Women to make women eligible for jury service. Donaldson did not believe women should be compelled to serve and spoke out against the measure at a Judiciary Committee hearing crowded with nearly two hundred supporters.

Donaldson may have been a women's rights pioneer, but her policy views tended to be more traditional. "I have never asked a concession of the male members and I hope the other women will adopt the same course," she would later say.[95]

Rumors abounded that some of the advocates would boycott the history-making afternoon session to rebuke Donaldson for what they felt were her insufficiently progressive views. In the end any lingering bad feelings were overcome by the significance and pride in Donaldson's recognition and the women filled the overflowing galleries to show her their support.

Donaldson plowed through the remainder of the House docket without incident. The afternoon's business included a Senate amendment on the hunting of deer on state forest reservations and a House bill governing the use of political designations in Boston city elections. Two roll calls were held, with several speeches and plenty of debate sprinkled in between.

Her colleagues and the press accounts offered high marks for her performance and poise. "The previous question was moved, and she uncompromisingly shut off debate at the proper time and put the question," one newspaper recounted. "Years of training as a 'school ma'am' stood 'Madame Speaker' in good stead, for she went through the business on the House calendar without a sign of nervousness and with a degree of assurance seldom displayed by men substituting for the speaker," wrote another.[96]

With the business of the House completed a motion to adjourn was accepted and Donaldson banged her gavel at 4:26 p.m. to end the session. Another burst of applause erupted as she laid down her gavel and stepped down from the rostrum as she was quickly surrounded by a jubilant mass of colleagues and supporters eager to bask in the history making day.

Donaldson's barrier-breaking session made national news and was covered in the press from Maine to California. The *South Bend Tribune* ran an austere looking photo of Donaldson with a brief news article on their front page, as did the *Burlington Free Press* and the *Minneapolis Star*. "She wields a snappy gavel," quipped the *New Britain Herald*,[97] while a Texas newspaper described her wielding "a hard-boiled gavel." [98] The *Los Angeles Times* published a photo of Donaldson holding her gavel in a news photo collage. Lengthier accounts were published in the Boston area press including the *Boston Daily Globe* and *Boston Herald*, which carried a large front-page photo of Donaldson standing at the House rostrum surrounded by men.

By the next day Donaldson was back in her regular House seat in the third division. Her new-found celebrity brought more speaking invitations and meeting requests, but her typical modesty and conservative outlook remained unchanged. She was a frequent guest at local Rotary and women's club meetings and occasionally travelled around to support other women running for public office.

Her electoral success was cited by other women who aspired to ride her coattails. One local candidate from Quincy touted Donaldson's accomplishments and admonished her local supporters to follow in the city of Brockton's footsteps in supporting a female candidate. "You, men of Quincy, if Brockton could put a woman in office, you can do no less," she said.[99]

Donaldson had a medical issue with her eye that sidelined her for a short time, but she returned to work soon thereafter and ran for a third term later that fall. Her successful campaign cost $58.16.[100] This time she was one of three women elected to serve in the legislature. The ranks of women increased slowly and by her fourth term she was one of five female House members.

By 1930, the partisan tides had shifted and the city of Brockton was no longer a Republican stronghold. Donaldson and her fellow Republican, in what was now the Ninth Plymouth District, were swept out of office and replaced by a pair of Democrats. It was part of a broader trend that saw Democrats also take the governor's office and a U.S. Senate seat.

In 1937, at the age of eighty-five, Donaldson broke her hip in a fall and later died of her injuries. The first line of her obituary notice heralded her as the first woman ever to preside over the Massachusetts House of Representatives.[101]

SUPER SUFFRAGIST SUSAN FITZGERALD

Long before she joined Sylvia Donaldson as a trailblazing state legislator casting votes inside the State House, Susan Fitzgerald was fighting for her right to vote outside the state capitol. Fitzgerald was already a well-known women's suffrage leader by 1911 when she helped lead a "Votes for Women" campaign that included a demonstration at the State House following a public hearing on suffrage legislation.

Years before she was elected as a state legislator, Susan Fitzgerald was speaking out in support of women's suffrage at the State House. *Library of Congress.*

It was a chilly Thursday evening in February when supporters gathered for the Committee on Constitutional Amendments hearing after marching through Boston Common. A capacity crowd filled the hearing room and overflowed into an adjacent room. Others congregated outside on the front steps of the State House or rallied in nearby Ford Hall. The thirty-nine-year-old Fitzgerald, who made a "businesslike appearance in dark grey cloth" [102] according to one newspaper account, helped manage the speakers and the overflow crowds.

On the docket were a pair of bills that would add a state constitutional amendment giving women the right to vote. The hearing lasted nearly three hours and Fitzgerald and other pro-suffrage leaders shuffled between the hearing room, the State House steps and Ford Hall to address the crowds and share updates. Hundreds of women, and some men, huddled outside in their winter coats to listen and offer support.

At one point Fitzgerald stood on the State House steps and addressed the flock of supporters who were not able to squeeze inside the room. The sound of fife and drum rang in the air while she spoke of their "Votes for women" campaign. Fitzgerald and her fellow suffragists were quite pleased by the showing. For the first time, a sizable number of men had joined their cause.

A smaller contingent of anti-suffrage leaders also attended and testified at the hearing. They argued that most women preferred to attend to their "home duties" and did not really want the burden of voting or engaging in partisan activities. "They even begrudge the time required to come to this hearing," claimed the leader of one anti-suffrage group.[103]

The hearing was dominated by the pro-suffrage crowd, however, and they applauded vigorously at the various speakers who stood up to testify before the legislative committee. Among them was Sylvia Pankhurst, an Englishwoman and outspoken suffragist, who stirred the crowd with her powerful remarks.

"They say women don't want to vote. But they said the slaves didn't want to be freed," said Pankhurst.[104]

The impassioned speeches continued until nearly eleven o'clock in the evening when the hearing concluded, and the boisterous crowd eventually dispersed. The following day's coverage of the "Votes for Women" rally led the news in most Boston newspapers.

Fitzgerald continued her advocacy, both as a leader of the Massachusetts Woman Suffrage Association, and as a candidate herself. Later that year she ran for a seat on the Boston School board, one of the few public positions for which women were allowed to vote at the time. Her platform included plans to ensure more public participation and put an end to secret sessions.

Ultimately Fitzgerald lost the election in early 1912 and the women's suffrage legislation was also defeated—but the seeds of change had been planted, and she was later elected to the Massachusetts House of Representatives.

Chapter 18

A LINCOLN LIKENESS
(1928)

When I was little the boys all called me 'Abe.'

FEBRUARY 16, 1928: No, it wasn't the "Great Emancipator" glaring back from the steps of the State House, but rather Lincoln H. Caswell, a Methodist minister from New York and noted Abraham Lincoln impersonator.

When he wasn't writing sermons, Caswell capitalized on his striking resemblance to the former president by touring around the country and performing reenactments of the Gettysburg Address and other famous Lincoln speeches, using the funds raised to help needy parishioners.

Caswell stopped by the State House while he was in town for a lecture to the delight of some astonished employees and visitors. Wearing a plug hat, black shawl and cowhide boots, he held court in the Hall of Flags, standing next to a display of tattered Civil War flags, while the room filled up with curious onlookers.

One observer described Caswell as a "tall, raw-boned man with whimsical mouth and the sad tired eyes of Lincoln, a seeming embodiment of the Civil War president."[105]

Outside the State House, a crowd estimated at five hundred people collected near Beacon Street to watch. Caswell paused on the State House steps to share a story with some local children and then eventually left in a taxi. He was due to return again over the weekend for a talk at a local Congregational church.

Caswell was passionate about Lincoln's teachings and approached his performances and educational work as if it was a divine mission. His father had named him after the former president long before it became clear that he shared a striking physical similarity and Caswell had grown up filled with admiration for Lincoln.[106]

"When I was little the boys all called me 'Abe,'" he once recalled.[107]

Lincoln Caswell, renowned Abraham Lincoln impersonator, visited the State House in 1928. *University of Massachusetts at Amherst Special Collections.*

Chapter 19

A REVOLUTIONARY TERCENTENARY (1930)

*For we must consider that we shall be as a City
upon a hill. The eyes of the people are upon us.*

OCTOBER 20,1930: Puritan leaders held the first session of the Great and General Court of the Massachusetts Bay Colony in Boston on October 19, 1630.[108] Three hundred years later, some of their progeny now celebrated the historic anniversary with a special session of the state legislature—still formally known as the General Court.

Speaker Leverett Saltonstall, a descendant of one of the original members, presided over the joint session along with Senate President Gaspar Bacon. Patriotic melodies from a cadet orchestra filled the crowded House chamber.

"Massachusetts has ever gone forward. She has been a pioneer in all movements for the betterment of her people," Senator Bacon told the members gathered for the solemn occasion. "She stands today in the forefront of the states in the union, a leader in administration, a leader in legislation, a leader in the dispensation of justice."[109]

The speakers also included Governor Frank Allen and Chief Justice Arthur Rugg. A host of former legislators, mayors, and other dignitaries from all corners of the state were also in attendance—although perhaps the most well-known living General Court alumnus was not.

Reverend Abbott Peterson, Monsignor M.J. Splaine, former President Calvin Coolidge and Herbert Parker, chairman of the Massachusetts Bay Colony Tercentenary Commission, lead the procession from the State House to the Boston Common for the Tercentenary in July of 1930. *Boston Public Library*

Former President Calvin Coolidge, who had served as a state representative, state senator, lieutenant governor, and governor before his time in the White House, sent his regrets. Coolidge had attended other tercentenary celebrations earlier in the year, however, including an elaborate parade and gathering on the Boston Common in July.

The broader historical significance of the Massachusetts Bay Colony founding in 1630 was embraced with patriotic fervor throughout the year. It also coincided with the 150th anniversary of the adoption of the Massachusetts state constitution, a model for the United States Constitution.

State leaders had planned ahead for the tercentenary and appointed a special commission two years earlier to devise a series of observances. The commission formulated an ambitious agenda with equal parts pageantry, patriotism, historical observance, and marketing, to highlight the state's role as the shrine of American democracy. The Commission planned for a budget of $105,000 and expected eight million additional auto tourists to visit the state over the course of the year.[110]

Governor Allen helped kick off the commemoration with his inaugural message to the legislature delivered in January. Allen invoked John Winthrop, the Colony's first governor, who had famously delivered a sermon during his voyage across the Atlantic setting forth the Puritan settlers' divine mission. "For we must consider that we shall be as a City upon a hill. The eyes of the people are upon us," Winthrop wrote.[111] Allen leaned in heavily to the same historical themes:

> *"Long before Voltaire and Rousseau had fired the world with their theories of equality, the Puritan fathers had planted the seeds of a government which was to lead the world in its march toward democracy. From the very beginning the principle of representative government has been the keystone in our political arch. The New England town meeting has demonstrated the actual operation of democratic principles in pure form. Our great Republic, whose birth altered the entire course of human events, owes its existence to the leadership of Massachusetts in the great struggle for American independence."*

After more speeches, handshaking, and pageantry the State House ceremony wrapped up with a public reception in the Hall of Flags. State leaders were pleased with the day's events, as well as the broader results of the tercentennial celebrations. Over the course of the year there were nearly two thousand different events across 250 towns in Massachusetts, attracting nearly ten million people.[112] Some attempted to include Native American perspectives—including one event featuring a Wampanoag leader descended from Massasoit—but for the most part organizers glossed over, or ignored entirely, the negative impacts of Puritan colonists in favor of a more idealized origin story.

Members of the Tercentenary committee present a framed copy of the 300th poster to Governor Allen (third from left). *Boston Public Library.*

The nation had recently been jolted by a major stock market crash, a series of bank closures, and spiking unemployment and so the tercentennial was viewed as salve in a "time of psychological letdown and financial depression."[113] For one year at least the effort seemed to have worked. While Massachusetts, like the rest of the nation, was facing an increasingly bleak fiscal forecast, the tercentennial observances helped keep the state treading water financially. A report released the following year estimated that the year-long 300th birthday party cost the state a little less than two million dollars and generated forty-seven million dollars in economic activity.

THE CASE OF MRS. SHERMAN'S STRAY PIG

While the membership of the General Court in 1930 did not look all that different from 1630—it remained predominately white, male, and protestant—the institution itself had undergone a dramatic transformation. The original General Court was a unicameral body that met quarterly to administer laws, elect officers, and render judgements under the royal charter—that is until a dispute over a stray pig changed history.

When the General Court first met on North American soil in 1630, its members, known as assistants, were elected by the freemen (loyal church members) of the colony. The wealthy Puritan assistants wielded a great deal of power and as the number of colonists granted freeman status increased, disputes arose over taxes and the administration of government. Soon the freemen from each town began to elect deputies to send to the General Court and act on their behalf.

The assistants and the deputies continued to meet as one assembly until 1644 when they split into separate bodies: an upper branch known as the Council of Assistants and a lower branch known as the House of Deputies— the precursor to our modern Senate and House. The new House of Deputies first assembled on May 29, 1644, and the next day elected William Hawthorne of Salem as their first speaker. The momentous development in representative democracy that would become a bedrock principal of the future nation can be largely credited to Mrs. Elizabeth Sherman of Boston and her stray pig.

The story began around 1636 when Mrs. Sherman accused Captain Robert Keayne, a local merchant, of capturing and killing her husband's stray pig, described as a white sow with a ragged ear and a black spot under the eye. [114] Mrs. Sherman, a mother of five daughters, was a local housekeeper and cook of modest means. Her husband, Richard, was not present in the colony during the incident and may have been back in

England, or already deceased. Captain Keayne was one of the founders of the Ancient and Honorable Artillery Company and known as a shrewd businessman.[115]

Keayne disputed the story and claimed that a pig with similar markings had wandered onto his property. He had attempted to find the rightful owner and when that was not successful, he kept and fed the sow along with his own. About a year later Keayne slaughtered one of his pigs and Mrs. Sherman came forward to claim that it was her lost pig. There were conflicting accounts as to the description of the animal and Keayne denied that the slaughtered sow was hers.

When Keayne refused to make good on the pig, Mrs. Sherman took her cause to the church elders. They investigated the claim, interviewed witnesses, and eventually ruled in Keayne's favor. Mrs. Sherman was not easily deterred, however and she decided to bring her case to the local court in Boston. Following a hearing, the jury ruled in Keayne's favor and awarded him court costs in the amount of three pounds.

Despite the setbacks, Mrs. Sherman continued to level accusations at Keayne and plead her case among the townspeople. He responded by bringing an action against her, claiming that she was slandering him with the

An 1897 cartoon in the *Boston Globe* depicts the story of Mrs. Sherman making an appeal for her stray sow before the colonial governor. *Boston Globe.*

THE WIDOW SHERMAN ACCUSES CAPT KEAYNE BEFORE THE GOVERNOR.

stolen sow claims. The jury found in Keayne's favor again and assessed her twenty pounds in damages. While the facts of the dispute favored Keayne, public sentiment seemed to side with Mrs. Sherman. The exorbitant court costs assessed against her contributed to a narrative that the wealthy magistrates were piling on a downtrodden woman.

Time passed and Mrs. Sherman later decided to petition the General Court for relief, with help from her tenant, a young English merchant. The same class-based divisions were mirrored among the membership of the General Court. The assistants, mostly wealthy landowners themselves, sided with Captain Keayne—while the deputies, who represented the townspeople, were more sympathetic to Mrs. Sherman's plight.

Governor John Winthrop.
New York Public Library.

When the General Court voted in 1642 after seven days of session, the assistants supported Captain Keayne by a 7 to 2 margin. The deputies voted 15 to 8 for Mrs. Sherman, with seven abstentions. Thus, the overall vote was 17 to 15 in support of Mrs. Sherman's claim that the pig had been unduly taken from her by Captain Keane.[116] Case closed, right?

Wrong. The assistants asserted that since a majority had voted against Mrs. Sherman, they negated the vote of the deputies, and thus her case could not prevail. A fundamental premise was in contention. Did a vote require the majority of both the deputies and the assistants—or just a majority of the entire body? In other words, could one group negate the vote of the other?

It was not the first time the issue had arisen, but the dispute over Mrs. Sherman's stray pig brought the issue center stage. A protracted debate about the "negative voice" ensued, which was detailed in colonial records kept by Governor John Winthrop. He sided with the assistants, though later tried to offer a more conciliatory approach.

> *I understand divers have taken offence at a writing I set forth about the sow business; I desire to remove it, and to begin my year in a reconciled estate with all.[117]*

The "sow business" as Winthrop called it, eventually resulted in a compromise. The assistants and the deputies would henceforth meet as separate bodies. Each would have veto power over the other. The bicameral legislature was born. It's not clear if Mrs. Sherman ever got compensated for her pig, but her persistence paid off and Keayne did agree to remit the court damages.

In the end, the lost pig was the republic's gain.

Chapter 20

'FLYING DAUGHTER' WELCOMED HOME (1932)

It also has been reported that
I killed a cow in landing!

J**UNE 29, 1932:** The red and white low-wing monoplane landed at the East Boston airfield on a warm Wednesday morning in June. For Amelia Earhart, the short flight from New York was quite unremarkable when compared to her history making trans-Atlantic flight one month earlier.

In May, she'd become the first woman, and the first person since Charles Lindbergh five years prior, to fly solo nonstop across the Atlantic. Now she was

Amelia Earhart waves from the front steps of the State House during a reception held in her honor. *University of Massachusetts at Amherst Special Collections.*

returning to Boston, where she had once worked as a social worker, to be honored with a ticker-tape parade.

The procession, replete with marching bands and honor guards, began at the airport and wrapped through downtown Boston to City Hall and up to the State House. The streets and sidewalks filled with exuberant spectators eager to catch sight of the famous aviatrix who had captured the public imagination ever since her first flight across the Atlantic in 1928 as a crew member.

Earhart was presented with a bouquet of pink roses on her arrival in Boston and a reception was held on the front steps of the State House shortly before noon. Afterwards, she was ushered into the governor's office and awarded a gold medal affixed with an airplane symbol and platinum wings, similar to what was given to Lindbergh after his historic flight.

Governor Joseph Ely was in Chicago at the time, attending the Democratic National Convention, but he prepared a written statement praising Earhart which was read aloud during the brief ceremony: "Your unwillingness to rest satisfied with achievements which would be for most human beings more than enough for one lifetime, your determination to do regardless of the odds against you," he wrote "are characteristic of those daughters of Massachusetts, whom ... the Commonwealth has delighted to honor."[118]

After departing the State House, Earhart was joined by friends and family for a city luncheon and later attended a dinner banquet at Copley Plaza. She shared anecdotes from her recent history-making flight from Newfoundland to Northern Ireland and charmed the audiences with her grace, modesty, and sense of humor.

Earhart returned to Boston after her history making trans-Atlantic flight in 1932. *University of Massachusetts at Amherst Special Collections.*

At one point Earhart even had some fun debunking a few flights of fancy that had taken root about her trans-Atlantic voyage. "It also has been reported that I killed a cow in landing," she recounted. "If so, I didn't know about it unless the cow died of fright from the noise of the plane!"[119]

FLIGHTS OF FANCY

The public's growing fascination with aviation was frequently on display at the State House between the First and Second World Wars, an era often known as the Golden Age of Flight. In addition to Amelia Earhart and Charles Lindbergh, the State House welcomed a number of other pioneering pilots, including "Wrong Way" Douglas Corrigan, a trio known as the Bremen Flyers, and Ruth Elder, a barrier-breaking pilot and aspiring actress.

THE BREMEN FLYERS. In the spring of 1928, a month before Amelia Earhart's first trans-Atlantic flight, a trio of German and Irish fliers made the journey in reverse, successfully completing the first nonstop flight from Europe to North America. Captain Hermann Koehl, Baron Günther von Huenefeld, and Major James Fitzmaurice departed from Ireland and landed in Labrador in a Junkers W 33 monoplane called the "Bremen." The Bremen Flyers, as they were known, were invited to the State House on May 20, 1928, where Governor Alvan Fuller presented the men with medals to recognize their accomplishment.

Governor Fuller recognizes the Bremen Flyers. *Boston Public Library Leslie Jones Collection.*

ACTRESS AND AVIATRIX. Ruth Elder, a twenty-three-year-old pilot and aspiring actress, also had ambitions to fly across the Atlantic. In October of 1927, she became the first woman to attempt a transatlantic flight, taking off from New York and heading for Paris, France. Elder's plane developed an oil leak however and she and her partner had to make an emergency water landing. Despite the failed attempt, Elder set a new endurance flight record and became a celebrity.

She toured the State House on March 5, 1928, visiting the Hall of Flags and the governor' office, where she caused a mini-stir by declaring that Governor Fuller was "perfectly lovely" and promised to vote for him if he ran for president.[120] She later starred in a pair of Hollywood motion pictures.

Ruth Elder. *Boston Public Library Leslie Jones Collection.*

'WRONG WAY' CORRIGAN. Douglas Corrigan was an aircraft mechanic turned pilot who earned fame in 1938 for his "accidental" transatlantic flight in a rebuilt aircraft reclaimed from a junkyard. Corrigan originally wanted to fly from New York to Ireland, but local authorities deemed his plane unsafe for a trans-Atlantic voyage and rejected the request. So instead, Corrigan filed a flight plan that would take him west back to Long Beach, California. Soon after takeoff, however, his plane veered in the opposite direction and then vanished behind the clouds.

The next day Corrigan landed safely in Dublin, Ireland. He claimed that the weather had caused a navigational malfunction and sent him flying in the wrong direction. It seemed

Douglas "Wrong Way" Corrigan came to Boston and was celebrated with a ticker tape parade and a visit with Governor Charles Hurley at the State House. *Boston Public Library Leslie Jones Collection.*

an unlikely claim, but Corrigan stuck to his story and quicky earned the moniker "Wrong Way" Corrigan. With the exception of some unamused aviation overseers, Corrigan's escapade drew wide fanfare and he was feted upon his return to the United States.[121]

POLAR EXPLORER

Exploration was also a recurring theme during this era. When Rear Admiral Richard Byrd pulled into Boston's South Station on the afternoon of June 27, 1930, the temperatures were climbing into the low eighties—a far cry from the conditions the famed explorer faced during his expedition of the Antarctic. Soon after his return from the South Pole, Byrd visited Boston and was given a hero's welcome, including an elaborate parade. Governor Frank Allen honored the pioneering admiral and his colleagues with a ceremony on the front steps of the State House. The front of the building was draped with American flags and a massive banner welcoming Byrd and his valiant crew. Byrd brought his family along, including his beloved mascot, Igloo, a now famous white fox terrier that had accompanied him on the history making expedition.

Admiral Richard Byrd with Igloo. *University of Massachusetts at Amherst Special Collections.*

Chapter 21

THE CASE OF THE COD CAPER (1933)

Steal all the Cabots, if you must,
but spare our cods—in cods we trust!

APRIL **26, 1933:** Posing as tourists, the thieves entered the State House late in the afternoon and headed for the fourth-floor gallery overlooking the House chamber. Two of the men wore white saddle sport shoes and one carried an unusually long flower box under his arm that appeared to be filled with Easter lilies. One of the

State House Library.

men was at least six-feet tall with curly brown hair and a polo coat and another was described as short and portly. A fourth man waited outside in an automobile.

The House adjourned its regular business for the day at 5:18 p.m. and the men hid behind seats in the gallery while legislators, clerks, and staff filed out of the room below. When the coast was clear, the men reached high over the railing and cut two threads of metal wire that held an historic ornamental fish made of pine wood—better known as the Sacred Cod.

The nearly five-foot long replica painted in silver signified the importance of the fishing industry to Massachusetts and had hung in the chamber since 1895. The tradition dated back even longer and earlier versions of the wooden codfish were on display in the Old State House well before the American Revolution.

A committee tasked with reporting on the history of the "sacred emblem" in the late nineteenth century described the symbol in solemn terms:

> *"Let us take it in reverence and honor, and place it on high as one of the proudest decorations of this great hall; and let it remain there so long as this State House shall stand, a memorial of the Pilgrim, his privations and simplicity; an emblem significant of the hardiness, courage and faith of those who dare and defy the seas, and daily telling of the great and surpassing glories of Massachusetts and her sons."[122]*

After cutting it down the thieves carefully stowed the wooden fish in the long flower box. Bits of greenery fell out in the process and were later discovered on the House gallery floor along with a torn envelope. Once the

The theft of the Sacred Cod from the House chamber in 1933 drew national attention. *Boston Public Library Leslie Jones Collection.*

Sacred Cod was hidden away, the men surreptitiously exited through the adjoining press gallery and made their way back downstairs.

The thieves had scoped out the building the day before and studied the routines of the court officers and doorkeepers to facilitate their getaway. It was about six o'clock in the evening and the sun was just setting on Beacon Hill when they furtively exited the building via a side entrance by Ashburton Street.

The theft was discovered by a watchful guard later that evening around eight o'clock and the state police were quickly notified, along with the sergeant-at-arms and building superintendent. Police detectives inspected the gallery and scrutinized the walls and railings for fingerprints. A systematic search of the entire building was also conducted. Few leads were found.

The theft of the Sacred Cod quickly captured the public's attention and sparked numerous offers to help. Officials in Barnstable County held an emergency meeting and wired a message to the governor offering to loan their own sacred Cape Cod codfish to the legislature until the Commonwealth's "immortal and sacred" codfish was recovered.[123]

Plenty of anonymous tips, fishy rumors, and red herrings also flooded in. One lead took police north of Boston to the city of Lynn, where a Boston University student was mistakenly suspected of involvement. Another tipster claimed that the fish was being spirited away to New York by airplane, which led to one unlucky college student being deplaned, questioned, and searched by police until it was discovered he was the victim of a practical joke.

Police also conducted a search along the banks of the Charles River, mistakenly believing that the thieves might have intended to return the cod to its natural habitat. Another fishy report claimed that the Sacred Cod could be found in a five-foot box in the basement of the Massachusetts Institute of Technology. When a search was conducted a box was indeed found but it contained only an unfortunate minnow.

Some leads did pan out. Police were able to track down a florist in Cambridge who remembered selling a large flower box to a young man matching eyewitness accounts. The lead also matched up with the evidence of laurel sprigs discovered in the gallery.

The trail of suspicion quickly led back to Harvard Square. It was well known that students at the *Harvard Crimson* and the rival *Harvard Lampoon* often committed elaborate pranks. Accusations quickly flew between the two feuding student publications, accompanied by threats of expulsion from the college administration. At one point the *Crimson* claimed to have evidence of the *Lampooner's* liability and threatened to expose those involved if the fish was not promptly returned.

Two days after its theft from the State House, the Sacred Cod was returned to police, mostly unharmed. *Boston Public Library Leslie Jones Collection.*

Thomas Bligh, the lead police detective on the case, shared the belief that Harvard students were to blame for confiscating the cod. "It's probably the *Lampoon* boys," he told the Boston press.

"They think it's a prank. But it's not. It's serious."[124]

Two days after the theft, with pressure and accusations growing, a mysterious phone call was placed to Harvard Yard Police Captain Charles Apted around ten o'clock in the evening. "I was asked if I was interested in the Sacred Cod," he recounted. "I said I was."

Apted was given instructions on where to meet and that evening he drove to the rendezvous near the Chestnut Hill Reservoir. On arrival he spotted a car, described as a "roadster," with two men inside and no rear license plate. He approached, but the vehicle sped away along the darkened road.

Apted drove in pursuit for about twenty-five minutes until the roadster finally stopped on a side road. One of the men exited wearing a mask and unceremoniously handed over the five-foot cod. Before Apted could commit any details of the encounter to his memory, the man had returned to his car and sped away.

With the fish recovered, Apted immediately notified Detective Bligh and drove to his office later that evening to deliver the prized possession. By the following morning the Sacred Cod was back at the State House under the watchful care of the building superintendent. A few touch ups were necessary to fix three damaged fins but otherwise the cod was returned in good condition.

Later that morning the sacred symbol was restored to its rightful location in the House chamber, except this time it was hung a foot higher so as to prevent any future codnapping attempts.

Though *Harvard Lampoon* student editors were widely blamed for the theft, state police decided not to press forward with any charges once the fish was safely returned. The Sacred Cod story drew national attention and was featured on the front page of Boston newspapers for three straight days.

While ample prose was devoted to the case, the cod caper was also conveyed in poetry, including by one unidentified author:

Appeal for return of a Sacred Cod
"O shameless man,
O cruel thief!
Return our cod,
And ease our grief!

Oh, Massachusetts
There she stands
So pleadingly
With outstretched hands.

O, steal the Lowells,
If you wish,
But spare, O, spare
Our sacred fish.

Steal all the Cabots,
If you must,
But spare our cods —
In cods we trust!"[125]

COD CAPER, PART II

NOVEMBER 14, 1968: Another sacred cod-napping occurred some thirty-five years after the *Harvard Lampoon* heist. A diligent court officer discovered that the wooden fish was missing from its perch in the House Chamber on the morning of Thursday, November 14.

Authorities speculated that the thieves gained access via the adjoining press room some time after five o'clock the night before. A step ladder that was in use by workmen refurbishing the House chamber was found on the floor of the gallery.

As before, plenty of tips came in. One rumor claimed the cod would be unveiled at the next Harvard-Yale football game. This time students at the *Harvard Lampoon* immediately disclaimed any involvement. "We haven't exercised our sacred rights on the cod for some time now, we're too sophisticated for that kind of stuff," one student told the press.[126] Another anonymous caller said the filched fish was the work of ten students from the University of Massachusetts at Boston who planned to give it back during an upcoming campus ceremony.

While the theft was certainly taken seriously by police and State House officials, some Bay State salons adopted a more lighthearted take. When apprised of the missing cod, coming on the heels of a Nor'easter and in the absence of the governor, Lieutenant Governor Francis Sergeant joked, "That's too much for any lieutenant governor to handle. Even one who headed the division of Marine Fisheries."[127]

Francis Kelley, a former attorney general who had long championed the issue of public lotteries, used the theft to poke fun at the state's entrenched gambling interests. The Sacred Cod should be replaced by a plaque of a racing horse or bookie to represent the state's real largest industry, Kelley said facetiously—or not. "These powerful interests today control all the legal and illegal

The Sacred Cod went missing again in 1968 and was found after several days, hidden behind a door in the House chamber. *WHDH-TV.*

gambling," he said. "Perhaps this sacred codfish was rejuvenated by all the oratory and wiggled away in disgust."[128]

After three days of searching few leads had been found—until another anonymous call came in. A man who described himself as the father of a college student told police that the wooden fish remained in the State House and had been hidden in the basement.

The capitol police launched an immediate search of the basement area and then methodically covered each floor of the sprawling building until the cod was finally located on the third floor. As it turns out the sacred symbol never left the House chamber. It was found standing vertically on its tail behind a little used door leading to the chamber. Apart from a thick coating of dust the fish was unharmed.

"We had a line out for it all this time, and tonight we hooked it," said Capitol Police Chief Paul Doherty.

Chapter 22

A LOYALTY OATH (1935)

I do solemnly swear (or affirm) that I will support the
Constitution of the United States and the
Constitution of the Commonwealth of
Massachusetts...

JUNE 26, 1935: Governor James Curley took the oath of office in January. Now he wanted Massachusetts to join a growing number of states requiring schoolteachers to sign a similar pledge. Despite bitter opposition from educators, Curley signed the "loyalty oath" bill into law in June, surrounded by legislators, America Legion members, and anti-communist organizations.

The new law required Massachusetts public and private school teachers and college professors to swear allegiance in writing to the state and federal constitution. A carveout was added for exchange professors and visiting teachers from other countries. The new law, which passed the House by a 122-81 margin and on a voice vote in the Senate, went into effect in October.

The hotly contested measure was designed to address concerns of a growing "subversive" element in public education. "If they want so much to preserve the Constitution, why do they object to swearing allegiance to the Constitution?" asked lead sponsor Representative Thomas Dorgon of Dorchester at a public hearing. "Taking the oath of allegiance means swearing to uphold the freedom of speech that is guaranteed by the Constitution."[129]

Educators, including a group of influential college presidents, denounced the bill as unconstitutional. "You can't make people loyal by law," said one. "You cannot cast the imputation of disloyalty on educators and then expect them to help the laws," added another.

Attending the Harvard Commencement exercises days before, Governor Curley was subjected to criticism for his support of the measure. He fired back with charges that the universities were censoring patriotic films and limiting student access to military service recruitment.

"When such a situation develops, I believe that steps should be taken to inculcate the principles of Americanism in our youth," he said.[130]

The new law required teachers to sign the pledge and file a copy with their superintendent or college administrator, which would then be transmitted to the state commissioner of education. There was no enforcement mechanism or penalty in the original law, but educators who failed to take action could be barred from teaching.

Numerous attempts to repeal the teacher's oath law failed and the requirement remained on the books until it was invalidated by the courts in 1967.[131]

Governor James Curley signs the teacher's oath bill into law. *Boston Public Library.*

Chapter 23

BRINGING DOWN THE HOUSE—AND SENATE!
(1937)

*The whole affair was one of
unmixed, unmitigated rowdyism.*

MAY 28, 1937: With an orange piano, dance floor, and roller-skating team set to swing music, the scene was a vaudeville production worthy of an off-Broadway show—except this was the chamber of the Massachusetts House of Representatives.

In what had become an annual tradition, state lawmakers celebrated the final night of their 1937 legislative term, officially known as prorogation, with elaborate songs, jokes, and merriment. In addition to the singing and dancing, a mock trial was held in which one legislator was tried (and convicted) on charges of "insanity." The unlucky solon escaped his would-be jailers by racing up the aisle of the chamber all the while being pelted with moistened rolls of bathroom tissue—or "papers from the senate" as one spectator quipped.

For the lawmakers and their staff this "mock session," as it was known, was all in good fun; a way to let off some steam and pass the time while they waited for the formal process of engrossing the final batch of bills to officially end the term. Depending on the year, the level of entertainment ranged from the jocund to the ribald.

The tradition was not exclusive to Massachusetts; other state legislatures were also known to engage in end of session merriment. The origin of the mock session is uncertain, though it may have dated back to the British Parliament.

The end of the 1849 legislative term included a series of mock resolves that were read into the record while House lawmakers waited for the governor to formally end their session. They included resolves to annul the state constitution, refer to the governor as Moses, and abolish the state senate, but only the final resolve semed likely to come true: "Resolved, That we won't go home till morning."[132]

In 1852, news reports refer to the revival of an "old custom" of hosting a mock session following the state legislature's adjournment. It started off as a rather staid affair, however: The youngest member of the Senate presented the oldest member with a stout cane of Malacca wood mounted with agate and gold. This was followed with some good-natured joking.

Over the years the Massachusetts legislature elevated the mock session practice to a new art form, though for some critics it was more akin to putting the "rogue" back in prorogue. As early as 1855, some observers cast a critical eye on the revelry.

Representative John W. Lasell of Northbridge gets taken for a ride during the Legislature's Mock Session, which featured a vaudeville floor show in the House chamber with roller skating teams, piano and chorus.

"The usual 'mock session' was a disgusting affair," wrote one newspaper. "There is always danger that personalities and rough wit will degenerate into scurrility. In this occasion it was worse. The whole affair was one of unmixed, unmitigated rowdyism."[133]

Over the course of the next half century the tradition continued, waxing and waning based on the political currents of the time. In 1900, there was no mock session at all at the end of the term, though it was hardly a ringing endorsement of the legislature's accomplishments that year.

"There could be no parody so amusing as the real thing," quipped one writer.[134]

The fun had returned by 1902, when the last day of the mock session featured a full rag-time orchestra, singing choruses, and passage of "The Cat Bill." At one point a large group of House members marched en masse over to the Senate where they interrupted a poetry reading and began singing "How Dry I Am."[135]

The end of the Prohibition era seemingly coincided with another uptick in mock session activity and the 1934 term was noted as the "most frolicsome in years," with loud fireworks and plenty of liquor. A similar scene occurred two years later when fireworks were set off under the State House arch and unwittingly caused police to fear a bomb scare. Mock sessions continued with renewed vigor following the end of World War II.

In 1947, it was the Senate members who caused a commotion by parading into the House chamber and singing a merry rendition of "Take Me Out to the Ball Game" to close out the session. The song choice was intended as a jab at the House speaker who had criticized the Senate for adjourning early the night before so that members could get out of the sweltering Senate chamber and head over to Fenway Park to watch the Red Sox-Yankees game. (The Senate may have won the battle of wits, though the Red Sox lost the game.)

That year might have also signaled the ballgame for the formal custom of mock sessions in Massachusetts. In the face of growing criticism, legislative leaders soon cracked down on the practice. The bouts of marathon sessions, late-night lawmaking, and mischievous merriment would remain, of course, but for the roller skates, dance floors, and vaudeville acts, the show would not go on.

Chapter 24

WAR TIME MEASURES (1942)

The war has changed this job a lot.

OCTOBER 10, 1942: Governor Leverett Saltonstall, equipped with protective goggles and gloves, used a blowtorch to melt the ornamental black iron gates encircling the State House grounds. The ceremonial act was part of a broader effort to collect scrap metal for the war effort. A crowd watched as the governor melted the bars, including a metal plaque with Adolf Hitler's visage added for effect.

The 116-year-old State House fence, spanning about 300 feet, was expected to yield around thirty-five tons of salvageable metal for steel mills and foundries.[136] The governor pledged that every available ounce of scrap metal on state property would also be salvaged. A wooden fence would be installed to replace the traditional wrought iron one.

Governor Saltonstall takes a blow torch to an Adolf Hitler likeness. *Boston Public Library*

Governor Saltonstall takes a blowtorch to the iron fence encircling the State House as part of a war-time scrap metal drive. *Boston Public Library*

The scrapped fence was not the only change in support of the war effort. In March, Governor Saltonstall authorized the repainting of the State House dome out of fear that that the reflection from the gilded surface could make it a target to enemy aircraft. The historic dome, first coated with copper nearly hundred and forty years earlier, would be covered in a dull gray. A Revere contractor, C. Dale Garbutt, was awarded the job, which was expected to cost $595. In addition to two coats of battleship gray for the dome, the State House skylights were also painted black.[137]

The cosmetic changes at the State House during the war came along with a number of new policy matters to resolve, including oil shortages, new regulations for tire rationing, and war bond financing.

"The war has changed this job a lot," Governor Saltonstall later acknowledged.[138]

The State House dome was repainted a dull gray in 1942 to avoid attracting the attention of enemy aircraft. *Boston Public Library.*

Chapter 25

TAXING POLICIES (1947)

Hands off my paycheck!

MAY 20, 1947: The proposal for a new sales tax on the purchase of retail goods drew plenty of angry protesters to a public hearing at the State House. Governor Robert Bradford, a Republican, recommended a two percent tax to fund local aid and education. His plan,

A demonstration in front of the State House against a proposed sales tax on retail goods. *Boston Traveler.*

which would exempt food, medicine, gas, and services, was projected to raise an estimated sixty million dollars annually.

"This is not a spending program, it is a relief program," he explained.[139]

Still, it wasn't enough to quell the fears of some. Boston Mayor James Curley, a Democrat, opposed the levy, calling it a way of "soaking the poor," and instead advocated for a new corporate income tax. On the day of the hearing, picketers marched in front of the State House with signs reading "Hands off my paycheck."

The governor's sales tax plan was ultimately rejected by the legislature after lengthy debate. Ultimately, a state sales tax was not approved until 1966, when it was set at three percent.

The 1947 sales tax proposal was hardly the first to draw anti-tax activists to the State House. Armed with barrels and broomsticks, Republican activists celebrated the state tax filing deadline on April 15, 1952, with a picket in front of the State House. The trio was protesting a recent hike in the state income tax from 1.5 to 2.5 percent. The tax package, intended to close a budget deficit, was signed into law the previous November by Governor Paul Dever after being passed by the Democratic-controlled House and the Republican-controlled Senate. The final bill also increased the levy on capital gains income but nixed a plan to hike taxes on racetracks and out-of-state beer brewers. *Boston Herald.*

Chapter 26

DOUGLAS MACARTHUR RETURNS (1951)

He took Boston without a shot being fired.

JULY 25, 1951: In a triumphal speech to the Massachusetts legislature, General Douglas MacArthur made it clear that he did not, in fact, intend to fade away.

During his farewell address delivered three months earlier, MacArthur had famously quoted an Army ballad about old soldiers who didn't die, but just faded away. Now it was clear that, even if his military career might be over, the seventy-one-year-old general still had plenty left to say.

MacArthur arrived at the State House on a sunny and warm Wednesday evening in July after a whirlwind day touring the city by motorcade. The streets were jammed with thousands of spectators eager to see the celebrated war hero who had led troops in both world wars and more recently in Korea. Speculation now swirled that he might enter the political arena and possibly even

General Douglas MacArthur addresses a joint session of the House and Senate while state leaders look on, including Speaker Tip O'Neil. *Boston Public Library.*

challenge President Truman, who had unceremoniously relieved him of his command in April.

The general was known as a brilliant military tactician, but it was clear from the thunderous reception at every stop that he also knew how to orchestrate a charm offensive. "He took Boston without a shot being fired" one local newspaper quipped.[140]

After pulling up to the flag-draped front entrance of the State House under police escort, MacArthur and his wife Jean were greeted by Governor Paul Dever in the Hall of Flags. The general was then escorted to the governor's suite for a formal procession to the House chamber, where he was to deliver his remarks while his wife watched from upstairs in the speaker's gallery. MacArthur was dressed in a sparse suntan uniform adorned with five stars on each shoulder. He removed his iconic battle-battered gold-braid hat and left it in the governor's office.

Inside the chamber seating was at a premium and even some prominent figures like former Mayor James Michael Curley had to watch the proceedings via closed circuit television in the adjacent Gardner Auditorium. The speech was also broadcast live on Boston television and radio stations and drew national attention.

After a rousing standing ovation lasting nearly three minutes, MacArthur launched into his formal remarks shortly after nine o'clock. Sitting behind him were Governor Dever, House Speaker Tip O'Neil, and Senate President Richard Furbush, the lone Republican of the leadership troika.

A few Democratic legislators had given up their seats so their Republican colleagues could have extra room for guests, but the majority remained and most laid aside any partisan leanings to revel in the return of MacArthur, whose ancestral home was in Chicopee, Massachusetts, some ninety miles west of the capital.

MacArthur quickly dispelled any notion that his address would be merely ceremonial in nature. Though he came with "neither partisan affiliation nor political purpose," he made clear he would not be silenced by any leader and intended to speak his mind. "I shall raise my voice as loud and as often as I believe it to be in the interest of the American people," he said.

First on his agenda was the issue of communism, which he called an "evil force." He made clear that the battle against communism was not only to be fought on foreign soil, but also at home where he believed it was infiltrating the press, schools, and other institutions of public trust.

"There can be no compromise with atheistic Communism, no halfway in the preservation of freedom and religion. It must be all or nothing," he said.

MacArthur also raised the issue of government spending and what he called the "unconscionable burden" of taxation that was sapping the initiative and energy of the American people. He compared it to the days of the Boston Tea Party and blamed President Truman and others in "supreme executive authority" for their "reckless spendthrift policies."

"Worst of all, it is throwing its tentacles around the low income bracket sector of our society, from whom is now extracted the major share of the cost of government," he said.

Making matters worse, MacArthur argued, were misguided efforts under the guise of altruism to send large sums of foreign aid to other countries. "It is argued that we must give boundlessly if we are to be insured allies in an emergency. I reject this reasoning as an unwarranted calumny against well tested friends of long standing." A strong and prosperous United States was of more value to the continued survival of the free world than any sum of financial aid might be, he argued.

MacArthur devoted the bulk of his address to foreign policy, including the nation's role in the ongoing conflict in Korea, and was sharply critical of the Truman administration. He questioned the precept that military leaders owed their allegiances solely to the executive branch and reminded his audience about the authority of Congress in matters of war. If the armed forces were answerable only to the president, rather than the constitution and

General Douglas MacArthur is escorted into the House chamber to address a joint session of the legislature, joind by Governor Paul Dever and other state dignitarie. In his speech, MacArthur was sharply critical of U.S. foreign policy. *Associated Press.*

the country, he said it would be akin to a "Praetorian guard owing allegiance to the political master of the hour."

Though MacArthur said he did not question the president's authority to relieve him of his command, he did question the stated rationale behind it and claimed the administration had no coherent foreign policy when it came to Korea.

"We have been told of the war in Korea that it is the wrong war, with the wrong enemy, at the wrong time, and in the wrong place. Does this mean that they intend and indeed plan what they would call a right war, with a right enemy, at a right time and in a right place?" he asked.

While he was critical of the indecision, appeasement, and half measures that resulted in neither victory nor defeat, MacArthur made clear he was no warmonger. The ultimate goal must be to abolish war and lead mankind along the road to universal peace and prosperity, he argued.

MacArthur said he hoped his removal would spark a renewed interest among the American people to hold their political leaders accountable. He framed the issue in stark terms as a battle to save the soul of the nation.

> *"We stand today at a critical moment of history—at a vital crossroad. In one direction is the path of courageous patriots seeking in humility but the opportunity to serve their country; the other that of those selfishly seeking to entrench autocratic power.*
>
> *The one group stands for implacable resistance against communism; the other for compromising with communism. The one stands for our traditional system of government and freedom; the other for a socialist state and slavery.*
>
> *The one boldly speaks the truth; the other spreads propaganda, fear and deception. The one denounces excessive taxation, bureaucratic government, and corruption; the other seeks more taxes, more bureaucratic power, and shields corruption."*

MacArthur's address, which he read from a prepared text, lasted about forty minutes and was interrupted several times for cheers and applause. When he concluded with a simple "Good night," the members and guests offered a lengthy standing ovation—though some were taken aback by the fiery and political nature of the general's remarks.

The State House speech, and MacArthur's visit, dominated coverage in the Boston press, but also reached a national audience. Newspapers across the country splashed headlines about his attacks on the Truman administration and its foreign policy, stirring more talk of MacArthur's political ambitions. *Time Magazine* took note of the speech, and it even drew comment in the *London Times*.

"MacArthur chose a bipartisan Massachusetts legislature – a Republican Senate and a Democratic House – to lash out Wednesday night with one of the bitterest attacks on American policy since President Truman fired him from his Far Eastern commands," wrote the Associated Press, which speculated that with his speech MacArthur had thrown himself into the 1952 presidential fight, as either a candidate or campaigner.[141]

President Truman himself certainly took note of MacArthur's speech to the Massachusetts legislature. In a press conference the next day the president was asked about the general's pointed remarks.

"No comment" he replied.

NUCLEAR TEST BAN TALKS

The State House has been a forum for foreign policy debates on many occasions. In 1963, Undersecretary of State Averell Harriman addressed a joint session of the legislature. Harriman had recently returned from successfully negotiating a nuclear test ban treaty with Russia and used the visit to advocate for the formal ratification of the agreement by the U.S. Senate. The treaty had been in the works for a long time, but "I just happened to be around when Khrushchev was ready to come to an agreement," Harriman told his audience. [142] "Many ask, 'how can you believe Khrushchev?' and I say 'You have to believe him…the Kremlin leaders do not want war. They do not want to see what they have built destroyed…'"[143] Harrison also used the opportunity to decry cuts to the foreign aid budget by Congress.

Senate President John Powers, Governor Endicott Peabody (both seated) and Lt. Governor Francis Bellotti (standing) listen as United States Undersecretary of State Averell Harriman speaks on nuclear test ban talks in Moscow. *Boston Public Library.*

Chapter 27

THE LONE WALK (1953)

*I'm about the only man in the world
who hasn't a right in there.*

JANUARY 8, 1953: Outgoing Governor Paul Dever stepped out of the oversized front doors of the State House on a cold and gray Thursday afternoon to complete the traditional "lone walk" and return to private life—except he was hardly alone. More than five thousand cheering staff and supporters clogged the corridors, balconies, and nearby streets to watch the fifty-two-year-old Democrat make his departure after four years in the corner office.

After a bitterly fought election cycle Dever was touched by the unexpected show of support. As he descended the State House steps, he stopped halfway and turned to face the well-wishers surrounding him on the plaza. Dever did not say a word but instead lifted his pearl-gray fedora and nodded with a broad smile. The crowd roared back in approval.

After a handful of more brisk steps, Dever marched past the stone and wrought iron archway that marked the end of his ceremonial lone walk. He was greeted by family members and a new black Cadillac idling on Beacon Street. State police officers parted the crowd so that he could climb in the vehicle and make his departure. Moments later the boom of nineteen cannons echoed across the Boston Common, symbolizing the transition to a new administration.

Governor Paul Dever completes his "lone walk" in 1953. *Boston Public Library.*

The origin of the "lone walk" likely dates back to 1884, when then Governor Benjamin Butler was leaving office after losing his re-election bid. Butler, a Republican, was in the executive chamber for a reception with the incoming governor and other dignitaries. One by one the parties departed in a procession to the House chamber for the formal inauguration ceremonies and Butler was left standing all by himself with no role left to play. He found his assistant in the next room and nodded toward the chamber.

"I'm about the only man in the world who hasn't a right in there," he said.[144]

A wistful Butler waited in awkward solitude until the ceremony was completed. After a few last farewells he donned his hat and coat and walked quietly down the stairs to exit the State House. There were no crowds outside, just a horse carriage waiting to bring him to his hotel. Thus, a lone walk tradition was born—even if it was not yet labelled as such.

Although he served just a single one-year term in office, Governor Butler was also responsible for another notable gubernatorial transition tradition. Upon leaving office he gifted a handsome leather bible to his successor with a hand-written inscription:

"When I came into the Executive Chamber, a year ago, I could not find a copy of the holy scriptures. I suppose each Governor took it away with him. A friend gave me this. I leave it as a needed transmittendum to my successor in office, to be read by him and his successors each in turn."[145]

The passing on of Butler's bible and the "lone walk" tradition (occasionally the "long walk" or the "last walk") have continued in some form ever since. Some governors have departed office with their spouses, some with their lieutenant governor or key staff in tow, while others have taken the "lone" walk more literally.

Governor Butler's successor, Democrat George Robinson, also lamented the solitary nature of the transition when it was his turn to depart in 1887, though he at least had made the decision himself—unlike Butler, who was ousted by the voters. As the incoming governor and dignitaries filed out of the executive chamber Robinson was left alone. He was later interrupted by a visitor who asked why he remained in the executive chamber by himself while all the pomp and circumstance were taking place nearby.

Governor Benjamin Butler. *Library of Congress*

"The custom of the fathers has always been for the outgoing executive to take no part in the inauguration of his successor, and we do not deviate from that custom," he explained. "If a man were at all sensitive, and had been defeated, it would rather be gloomy for him to remain in a room so deserted; as for myself I do not mind it."[146]

Over time the quiet departure of the state's chief executive grew into the "lone walk" tradition known today. Governor William Russell, departing in 1894, "quietly made his way through the assemblage" and exited the State House."[147] In 1903, Governor Winthrop Crane was handed his coat and hat and "quietly left the chamber" with his son, descending the stairs and departing through the rear entrance where a carriage waited to drive him away.[148]

Two years later outgoing Governor John Bates left less quietly. He emerged from his office shortly after hearing the guns boom from the Common to signal the end of his term. "Well I can rest now," he quipped to a friend.[149] Bates donned his fur-lined overcoat and top hat and departed though the front entrance of the State House with a small entourage that included his stenographer and private secretary. He paused on the front steps for newspaper photographers to snap their pictures and then left via horse carriage.

Outgoing Governor James Curley attempts to depart with his new wife in 1937 following his "lone walk." *Jamaica Plain Historical Society*.

Governor Curtis Guild, a Boston Republican, chose a lower profile departure in 1909. He walked through the State House alone to a rear exit before the incoming governor had even returned from his inauguration ceremony. "It is the new governor's day entirely," he explained.[150]

Outgoing Governor Calvin Coolidge, known for his frugality with words, remained true to form and did not have much to say upon his departure in 1921—though he did make his exit through the front steps accompanied by at least eight staff members. Unlike many of his predecessors, Coolidge was not headed off into retirement or law practice, rather he had just been elected vice-president of the United States.

Governor Channing Cox also brought an entourage along for his departure in 1925. Perhaps eager to begin a planned trip to the West Coast that afternoon, Cox left the State House early, a few minutes before his successor was sworn in, and hopped into an automobile with his wife.

By the time Governor Frank Allen departed in 1931, the tradition had grown into a spectacle in itself, with large crowds gathered to watch the outgoing governor and his "remarkable ceremony of abdication."[151] The departure of his successor, Governor Joseph Ely, in 1935, similarly drew a large gathering of spectators.

Governor Charles Hurley leaves office in 1939. *Boston Public Library.*

Outgoing Governor James Curley added a new twist in 1937 by getting married on the morning of his departure. Curley returned to the State House two hours before the ceremonial hand-off to the incoming governor and then took his traditional lone walk, exiting through the front steps of the State House while a band played "Till we meet again." It was drizzling rain, but the colorful ex-governor was still enveloped by a crush of adoring crowds eager to wish him well. Curley's new bride waited for him in the car and the couple held a wedding reception later that day.

Governor Charles Hurley mostly stuck to tradition for his departure two years later, as did his successor Leverett Saltonstall. The popular outgoing governor took his "last march" in 1945, before heading off to Washington D.C. as United States senator-elect.

It was referred to as both a "long walk" and a "lone walk" for outgoing Democratic Governor Maurice Tobin in 1947, though just a "lone walk" for departing Republican Governor Robert Bradford in 1949, the first time the inauguration ceremonies were televised. Governor Christian Herter bundled up for his "long walk" on a bitterly cold day in 1957.

John Volpe was likely the first Massachusetts governor to give a repeat performance of the lone walk tradition. After losing his re-election bid to Endicott Peabody, Governor Volpe took his last walk down the State House steps in 1963. He was returned to office two years later however and served until 1969—when he took a cabinet appointment in the Nixon Administration and enjoyed another "lone walk" out of office.

The next governor to take a double dose of lone walks was Michael Dukakis who turned his initial departure in 1979 into a full-blown parade. The outgoing governor marched down the front steps of the State House

Governor John Volpe took the lone walk – twice.

with his family and a large contingent behind him—and didn't stop. Dukakis led the group down Beacon Street, past Government Center, and all the way to Quincy Market where they stopped at a Greek restaurant. Twelve years later, fresh off an unsuccessful campaign for the presidency, the outgoing governor reverted to a more traditional path to complete his lone walk and return to private life.

One of the quickest long walks on record was taken by Governor Jane Swift in 2003. After brief formalities, Swift departed with her husband and young children and reportedly descended the thirty-two front steps of the State House in less than a minute, before climbing into a green mini-van to return to her home in Williamstown.[152] By contrast, her successor, Governor Mitt Romney, lingered for nearly half an hour to cover the same terrain when it was his turn four years later.

In the annals of lone walks over a century and a half there could be many superlatives bestowed: Butler the first, Guild the quietest, Curley the most colorful, Dukakis the longest, Swift the briefest—but the most eventful may have been Foster Furculo. The forty-nine-year-old Democrat left office in 1961 after serving two terms. Furcolo took the traditional solitary walk down the front steps of the State House without incident; however instead of departing for home or vacation, Foster was promptly sent to the hospital for three days on the advice of his doctor for what was termed a "three-day routine check-up."

No doubt some commentators may have wondered if Furculo's "lone walk" would become his "final walk," but the governor recuperated and was soon back on his feet. The "lone walk" tradition continues in good health today.

Chapter 28

A 'FLOOD OF FILTH' (1954)

Your thinking has been warped by newspapers.

FEBRUARY 2, 1954: With growing concerns about an increase in juvenile delinquency, one ambitious Massachusetts state legislator decided that the "flood of filthy books" was to blame and proposed a new literary advisory board to scrutinize them.

At a legislative hearing at the State House before the Committee on Legal Affairs, state Senator John Collins brought along a bag of two dozen books he'd collected in support of his bill. Some of them dealt with themes such as homosexuality, birth control, and mental illness. His legislation would establish a seven-member council appointed by the Attorney General to inspect books and report on any "apt to corrupt youth."

"I can assure you each and every one of them is totally unfit for adult reading, let alone juvenile minds," Collins told the committee.[153]

The measure came at a time in the post-war, Cold War era when the country was still influenced by fears of communism. A proliferation of literary works challenging existing social norms and comic books with more mature themes also helped to fuel the controversy.

"This bill would be a welcome additional prevention of the abuse of freedom of the press by these perverted publishers who are more interested in the almighty dollar than they are in the youth of our country," Collins testified.[154]

State Sen. John Collins testifies at the State House on his bill creating an advisory board to review books and prevent the spread of "obscenity." *Boston Public Library*.

Not all were in agreement, however. At the hearing a bitter dispute erupted between advocates for the Collins bill and the Civil Liberties Union, which opposed the measure on constitutional grounds, calling it censorship. "Your thinking has been warped by newspapers," one attorney argued in opposition.[155]

For Collins, who had recently declared his candidacy for attorney general, the bill also proved a useful campaign tool. He charged that the present attorney general had done nothing to prevent the flood of "filthy" books in the state and made it a core part of his campaign platform.

The Legal Affairs Committee agreed with Collins and approved his bill after less than fifteen minutes of debate. Collins did not fare as well at the ballot box, however, and he lost his election to the incumbent attorney general later that year. He later bounced back and served two terms as mayor of the city of Boston, earning praise for his successful urban renewal policies.

Chapter 29

HEARST WARNS OF 'RED MENACE' (1955)

People are getting good and sick of all this hokum.

MARCH 31, 1955: William Randolph Hearst, Jr., scion of the famed newspaper tycoon, visited the State House in 1955, soon after returning from an extended visit to the Soviet Union, where he held a series of exclusive interviews with Russian leaders, including Nikita Khrushchev. Hearst warned the bicameral crowd gathered in the House chamber of the "Red Threat" presented by the "cold, ruthless leaders of communism" and advised them not to let their guard down.[156]

State leaders offered warm praise for Hearst during his visit and presented him with a plaque and congratulatory resolution. Hearst's "Report on Russia—Uncensored" series was published in his company's newspapers to much acclaim, and he would later earn a Pulitzer Prize for international reporting.

"Through his report he has brought great renown to the field of journalism," declared House Speaker Michael Skerry.[157]

During his remarks Hearst pledged to lend his support to a state commission conducting an ongoing probe of communism and "subversive" activities in the Commonwealth. The seven-member special commission had been appointed in July of 1953, building on prior committee work, and was chaired by state Senator Philip Bowker of Brookline.

William Randolph Hearst, Jr., editor-in-chief of Hearst newspapers, warned members of the Massachusetts legislature to be vigilant of the dangers of communism and the Soviet Union during his 1955 visit. *Boston Public Library.*

Three months after Hearst's State House speech, the Bowker Commission, as it was known, released its initial findings, which included the names and addresses of eighty-five "communist sympathizers." The 188-page report claimed credible evidence that the named individuals were current or former members of the Communist Party, which had formally been labelled a "subversive organization" under a 1951 state law.

The commission ordered two thousand extra copies of the report printed and took the unusual step of having the list read aloud in the Senate chamber, a measure designed to offer liability protection to press outlets that republished the names. Citing his poor eyesight, Sen. Bowker requested that fellow member Senator John Powers of Boston read the names.[158]

Senator Powers stressed that while the Commission had obtained the names of many suspected community sympathizers over the course of a two-year investigation, it chose to identify only those for whom it found there was credible evidence of involvement in specific communist affiliated organizations. This included New England Citizens Concerned for Peace, a communist front dedicated to a "Moscow-inspired 'peace' propaganda campaign for the benefit of Soviet Russia, the commission alleged.[159]

The report's authors took pains to distinguish their effort from highly-publicized investigations on the national stage led by Senator Joseph McCarthy of Wisconsin. McCarthy had recently been censured by the United States Senate following his multi-year crusade to root out alleged communist infiltration in government, including the U.S Army. After some early success—and a great deal of notoriety—McCarthy's embarrassing antics had worn thin, and he lost credibility in the eyes of many of his peers and the general public.

Broader fears of communist influence persisted, however, and Massachusetts legislators were intent on rooting them out. But where the McCarthy hearings focused on fear-mongering and division, the Commission assured that their work would be fact-based and deliberate. "Has this Commission erred, it has been neither through emotion nor haste,"[160] the authors claimed.

Most of the names in the report came as little surprise. Nearly all had previously appeared, or been subpoenaed, for questioning during one of the commission's numerous public hearings. Some individuals were already known to be past members of the Communist Party before it was officially outlawed.

Still, the explosive report dominated newspaper headlines from Boston to the Berkshires, including the *Boston American*, a Hearst-owned tabloid, which splashed the news across its front page in a sweeping sans serif font. A brief biographical sketch of each of the eighty-five individuals named was also published.

Some newspapers tracked down the accused to ask for comment. Many declined. Others proclaimed innocence. A few fired back at the commission.

"The state commission to investigate people with political ideas they differ with is attempting to revive the kind of hysteria in this Commonwealth that Joe McCarthy tried to do in our nation," charged Lynn resident James Bollen, a union steward who was named in the report. He urged labor groups to "stand up to these publicity-seeking politicians and tell them off."[161]

Another accused put it even plainer. "People are getting good and sick of all this hokum. They are smearing people without proof."[162]

While Hearst's papers applauded the investigators' work, some rapped it as an "undemocratic blacklist." It was a case of "government by fright," one newspaper declared. "There is little danger that the government of Massachusetts will be subverted by the Communists. There is considerably more danger that its traditions of free thought will be subverted...," the *Berkshire Eagle* editorialized.[163]

The Bowker Commission was undaunted. Through the end of the decade, the commission filed a dozen different reports, identifying more alleged

Senator John Powers shows off a Senate resolution presented to William Randolph Hearst, Jr. for his efforts reporting on the Soviet Union and top Russian leaders. During his visit, Hearst voiced support for a commission investigating communist influences in Massachusetts, led by Senator Phillip Bowker (left). *Boston Public Library.*

communist sympathizers and communist-affiliated organizations, including labor unions and educational institutions.

The legislature reauthorized the commission several times and Sen. Bowker remained active in the effort until he was eventually defeated for re-election in 1958. After a brief period of inactivity, the commission was revived again in 1960.

"The forces of subversion are still active, diligent and persevering. Communism is still alive and alert. In numbers the Party is small; in zeal its threat is vibrant," the newly-constituted commission declared.[164]

While the fears of communism continued to linger, the special commission was eventually disbanded for good. The state law outlawing the Communist Party in Massachusetts remains on the books today.[165]

Chapter 30

GLEASON PLAYS BIT PART IN BEANO BROUHAHA (1959)

Oh, it's a game.

SEPTEMBER 8, 1959: When actor and comedian Jackie Gleason arrived in Boston to promote his new pre-Broadway musical, few would have guessed he'd also play a cameo role in the latest political drama on Beacon Hill.

During his three-week stay in the city, Gleason was invited to address members of the legislature. The entertainer was well known for his starring role on *The Honeymooners* and *The Jackie Gleason Show* and was now featured in *Take Me Along*, a musical production of a Eugene O'Neill play opening at the Shubert Theatre.

Gleason visited the State House on Tuesday, September 8, 1959, and made brief remarks in both chambers, calling it "a great honor for a boy from Brooklyn." [166] His humorous quips entertained the members and overflow audiences filled with State House workers eager to hear from the famous actor.

In the state Senate, Gleason was presented with a gavel made of wood from "Old Ironsides" by Senate President John Powers, who was also in the midst of a campaign for mayor of Boston. But it was in the Massachusetts House where Gleason made the biggest impact—albeit inadvertently.

Playbill.com

The House was due to take up a controversial bill to legalize beano in Massachusetts. The bingo-like game of chance had been banned years earlier following a racketeering scandal that rocked the state. Supporters believed they now had the votes to pass the measure and bring beano back.

While standing at the rostrum after speaking to House members Gleason was asked if he intended to return to his lucrative television work after his current stage run ended. Spotting a copy of the pending beano bill, Gleason remarked, "Oh, it's a game—from the looks of this I might stay and run this instead of going back."

The offhand quip was interpreted by many as a jab against beano and its ties to less desirable elements. Soon thereafter the beano bill was narrowly defeated in the House by a five-vote margin. Many credited Gleason with an assist in its defeat.

Actor Jackie Gleason entertained legislators during an impromptu visit to the State House in 1959 and unwittingly played a cameo role in the latest political drama. *Boston Public Library.*

"Jackie Gleason seems to have done more to lick beano in Massachusetts than the urgent pleadings of many substantial citizens who have been given short hearing," one newspaper wrote.[167]

Gleason may have unwittingly helped pan beano in Massachusetts, but his stage musical fared much better. After a short series of Boston performances, *Take Me Along* had a successful run on Broadway.

Chapter 31

JOHN F. KENNEDY'S CITY ON A HILL (1961)

*For what Pericles said of the Athenians has
long been true of this commonwealth:
'We do not imitate—for we are a model to others.'*

JANUARY 9, 1961: The day began, like many before, with his traditional breakfast—two boiled eggs, generously buttered toast, and a pot of coffee—–in his cozy third-floor apartment on Beacon Hill, standing in the shadow of the State House. But for John F. Kennedy this was no ordinary day.

Kennedy's first official visit to the Massachusetts legislature had come fifteen years earlier, when as a young Navy Lieutenant returning from combat in the South Pacific, he was recognized during an informal House session. Tonight, the forty-three-year-old was returning to the State House as President-elect of the United States. The much-anticipated speech would be his

The John F. Kennedy Library.

Police officers Ignatius Rollka and Alphonso Carbone make security preparations at the State House in anticipation of the arrival of President-elect John F. Kennedy. *Boston Record American.*

first public address since the election and also marked his first return to the Bay State.

Kennedy arrived under the State House arch late in the afternoon on a cold and windy Monday, chauffeured in a white Lincoln Continental, along with a dozen police cruisers. He emerged wearing a dark blue suit and tie, but no winter coat or hat, and was still deeply tanned from a recent stay in Florida.

Lieutenant Governor Edward McLaughlin, a fellow U.S. Navy veteran, was tapped to formally greet the president-elect upon his arrival. He was joined by a select group of state lawmakers and a phalanx of secret service and capitol police numbering more than three hundred. A much larger assemblage of spectators gathered around the Mount Vernon Street entrance to catch a glimpse of Kennedy as he arrived.

After a visit to Governor John Volpe's office, Kennedy made his way to the House chamber to address the joint session of the legislature. The speech would cap off a day of activities in Boston, which included a visit to Harvard University and a meeting with the president of MIT. Later in the evening he was scheduled to fly back to New York City.

Legislators, judicial officers, and other state dignitaries and their family members crammed into the House chamber for the event, though the seating gallery was closed to the general public per orders of the Secret Service. One of the youngest spectators was two-and-a-half-year-old Richard Caples, who sat on the lap of his father, state Senator Richard Caples of Brighton.[168]

(One notable absence from the coterie of constitutional officers in attendance was state Treasurer John F. Kennedy. Kennedy, the treasurer, claimed he wasn't invited to the speech and instead planned to watch Kennedy, the president-elect, from home on his television. Apart from a similar name, the two men shared little in common. Treasurer Kennedy was a one-time stockroom supervisor who managed to thrice win election to state office despite hardly spending any funds—a feat most observers credited to his name, rather than his political skills.[169])

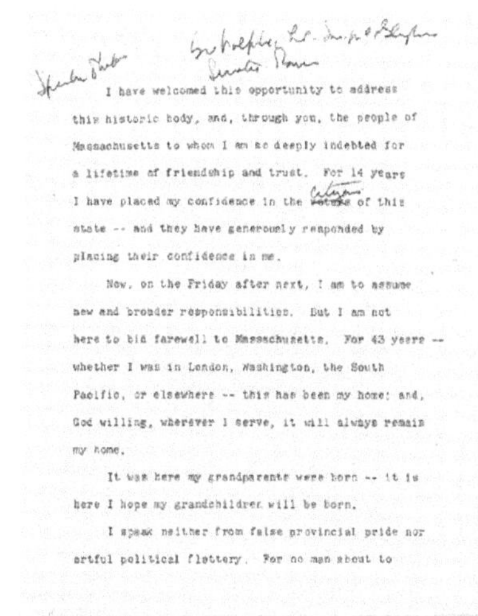

A page of Kennedy's original "City on a Hill" speech with handwritten notes added. *The John F. Kennedy Library.*

The president-elect arrived in the House chamber under tight security at 5:32 p.m. and was greeted with a standing ovation. He was escorted down the center aisle by the sergeant-at-arms, clad in a formal frock coat and top hat with gold and white mace. He paused along the way to shake the outstretched hands of lawmakers, greeting many by first name.

With House Speaker John Thompson and Senate President John Powers flanked to his rear, Kennedy stood at the dais. He was introduced by Governor Volpe, a Republican, who nonetheless bestowed high praise on the native son Democrat.

"Since the Pilgrims found their way to our shores, Massachusetts has produced men who have shown the way in building, under God, a great nation and government on the cornerstones of freedom, opportunity and equality," Volpe said in reference to Kennedy.[170]

When the thundering applause had died down Kennedy offered his greetings and then launched into his formal remarks, which lasted fewer than ten minutes:

> *I have welcomed this opportunity to address this historic body, and, through you, the people of Massachusetts to whom I am so deeply indebted for a lifetime of friendship and trust.*

For fourteen years I have placed my confidence in the citizens of Massachusetts—and they have generously responded by placing their confidence in me.

Now, on the Friday after next, I am to assume new and broader responsibilities. But I am not here to bid farewell to Massachusetts.

For forty-three years—whether I was in London, or in Washington, or in the South Pacific, or elsewhere—this has been my home; and, God willing, wherever I serve this shall remain my home.

It was here that my grandparents were born—it is here I hope my grandchildren will be born.

I speak neither from false provincial pride, nor artful political flattery. For no man about to enter high office in this country can ever be unmindful of the contributions which this state has made to our national greatness.

Its leaders have shaped our destiny long before the great republic was born. Its principles have guided our footsteps in times of crisis as well as in times of calm. Its democratic institutions—including this historic body—have served as beacon lights for other nations as well as for our sister states.

For what Pericles said of the Athenians has long been true of this commonwealth: "We do not imitate—for we are a model to others."

And so it is that I carry with me from this state to that high and lonely office to which I now succeed more than fond memories or firm friendships. The enduring qualities of Massachusetts—the common threads woven by the Pilgrim and the Puritan, the fisherman and the farmer, the Yankee and the immigrant—will not be and could not be forgotten in this nation's executive mansion.

They are an indelible part of my life, my convictions, my view of the past, and my hopes for the future.

Allow me to illustrate: During the last sixty days, I have been at the task of constructing an administration. It has been a long and deliberate process. Some have counseled greater speed. Others have counseled more expedient tests.

President-elect John F. Kennedy addresses the Massachusetts House and Senate on his first return to the Bay State following the November election. His ten-minute speech was broadly praised, and Kennedy worried it might overshadow his forthcoming inaugural address to be given in another ten days. *The John F. Kennedy Library.*

But I have been guided by the standard John Winthrop set before his shipmates on the flagship Arabella three hundred and thirty-one years ago, as they, too, faced the task of building a new government on a perilous frontier.

"We must always consider," he said, "that we shall be as a city upon a hill—the eyes of all people are upon us."

Today the eyes of all people are truly upon us—and our governments, in every branch, at every level, national, state and local, must be as a city upon a hill—constructed and inhabited by men aware of their great trust and their grave responsibilities.

For we are setting out upon a voyage in 1961 no less hazardous than that undertaken by the Arabella in 1630. We are committing ourselves to tasks of statecraft no less awesome than that of governing the Massachusetts Bay Colony, beset as it was then by terror without and disorder within.

History will not judge our endeavors—and a government cannot be selected--merely on the basis of color or creed or party affiliation. Neither will competence and loyalty and stature, while essential to the utmost, suffice in times such as these.

For of those to whom much is given, much is required. And when at some future date the high court of history sits in judgment on each one of us— recording whether in our brief span of service we fulfilled our responsibilities to the state—our success or failure, in whatever office we may hold, will be measured by the answers to four questions:

First, were we truly men of courage—with the courage to stand up to one's enemies—and the courage to stand up, when necessary, to one's own associates—the courage to resist public pressure, as well as private greed?

Secondly, were we truly men of judgment—with perceptive judgment of the future as well as of the past—of our own mistakes as well as the mistakes of others—with enough wisdom to know that we did not know, and enough candor to admit it?

Third, were we truly men of integrity — men who never ran out on either the principles in which they believed or the people who believed in them — men whom neither financial gain nor political ambition could ever divert from the fulfillment of our sacred trust?

Finally, were we truly men of dedication—with an honor mortgaged to no single individual or group, and compromised by no private obligation or aim, but devoted solely to serving the public good and the national interest.

Courage—judgment—integrity—dedication—these are the historic qualities of the Bay Colony and the Bay State—the qualities which this state have consistently sent to this chamber here in Beacon Hill in Boston and to Capitol Hill back in Washington.

And these are the qualities which, with God's help, this son of Massachusetts hopes will characterize our government's conduct in the four stormy years that lie ahead.

Humbly I ask His help in that undertaking—but aware that on earth His will is worked by men. I ask for your help and your prayers, as I embark on this new and solemn journey.[171]

When he finished, the capacity crowd rose to their feet and offered an enthusiastic ovation. After the applause subsided the joint session ended with a brief prayer from the Senate chaplain. Kennedy shook more hands as he dismounted the dais but did not linger long in the chamber. A planned post-speech reception in the Hall of Flags had been nixed by the Secret Service out of security concerns, so Kennedy hastily departed shortly before six o'clock and headed for Logan Airport.

In all, the president-elect spent fewer than sixty minutes inside the State House, but the impact of his brief visit was far-reaching.

Kennedy may have been using his speech to set a moral tone for his new administration—due to begin in ten more days—but it also contained a message for state leaders. A series of public corruption scandals had erupted over the previous year involving public works contracts and a federal investigation led to a number of indictments, including some state officials.

"The people of the state desperately need and would greatly appreciate a clarion call of some sort—an affirmation of the need for integrity and civic responsibility," the president-elect was advised several days before his speech.[172]

The message was delivered.

Kennedy's remarks were broadly praised, and his call for courage, dedication, and integrity in public service resonated well beyond Massachusetts. It may have been billed as his farewell address to the state legislature, but the speech quickly became known as his "City on a Hill" address.

Kennedy himself was pleased by the response. He would soon deliver an even bigger speech for his inauguration, and he wondered aloud if he had set too high a bar. "It's tough," he told a reporter. "The speech to the Massachusetts legislature went so well. It's going to be hard to meet that standard."[173]

Chapter 32

REVEREND KING STIRS AND INSPIRES (1965)

*For one who has been barricaded from the seats of
government and jailed so many times for attempting
to petition legislatures and councils, I can assure you
that this is a momentous occasion!*

APRIL 22, 1965: Representative Michael Haynes, a freshman lawmaker and ordained Baptist minister, marched up the aisle of the Massachusetts House chamber with joy in his steps.

It was late in the day on a cool and clear Thursday in April, a time when many lawmakers would normally have already decamped for their home districts, but today the room was packed. "There wasn't standing room in the

Rev. Martin Luther King. *Library of Congress.*

hall. A lot of legislators brought their whole families," he later recalled.[174]

Haynes was joined by a select group of legislators, including thirty-one-year-old Representative Michael Dukakis, a two-term lawmaker from Brookline, and their more senior colleagues Representative Royal Bolling, Representative Robert Quinn, and Senator Kevin Harrington.

Following tradition, in a bit of legislative pomp and pageantry, the legislators were formally tapped to proceed to the speaker's office and welcome a special guest to the joint session —Reverend Martin Luther King, Jr.

For Haynes, the honor carried special meaning. Haynes had become friends with Dr. King during his days as a theology student at Boston University when King often delivered guest sermons at the Twelfth Baptist Church in Roxbury, where Haynes also served as youth minister. The two had kept in close contact since and King had offered encouragement when Haynes decided to run for the state legislature.

Haynes in turn had played a key role in arranging for the civil rights leader to address the legislature during his scheduled two-day trip to Boston. The visit also included plans for a protest march from Roxbury to the Boston Common to call attention to the issues of school segregation and housing discrimination. A recently released report on racial imbalance in the Boston schools had put the issue squarely on the front burner.

The program for Martin Luther King's rally and march in Boston. *Northeastern University.*

In some corners of the city, King was met with a chilly reception— attempts to broker a meeting between King and Boston School Committee chairwoman Louise Day Hicks, a vocal opponent of school busing, broke down—but for the most part state leaders warmly welcomed the Nobel Prize-winning peace activist. For his part, Governor John Volpe greeted King soon after his arrival at the airport on Thursday morning and issued a proclamation in honor of "Martin Luther King Day" in Massachusetts.

In March, Volpe had dispatched his lieutenant governor to lead a state delegation to Selma, Alabama for a civil rights march with King in protest of the death of Boston Unitarian minister Reverend James Reeb. Reeb was brutally beaten by white segregationists while eating dinner at an integrated restaurant in Selma, where he had travelled after being inspired by King's call to service. The death of Reeb, a white man, garnered national attention and helped drive public opinion in support of federal voting rights legislation.

"James Reeb symbolizes the forces of good will in our nation," King said during his eulogy. "He was a witness to the truth that men of different races and classes might live, eat, and work together as brothers."

Representative Michael Haynes (left) helped arrange for Martin Luther King, Jr. to address the Legislature during his visit to Boston. Haynes had become friends with King during his days as a theology student at Boston University when King often delivered guest sermons. *Northeastern University.*

THE DEATH OF REEB, little more than a month prior, and the growing debate about busing and school segregation served as the backdrop for King's return to Boston. The visit was also an opportunity for King and his supporters to raise money for racial integration projects in the South—though, as one Boston faith leader declared, it was just as needed locally to call attention to "conditions of racial imbalance and slum housing."[175]

After a tour of several Boston schools and housing projects and a meeting with area religious groups, King arrived at the State House around four o'clock. Flanked by lawmakers, he entered the House chamber to a ringing ovation and proceeded to the rostrum where dozens of microphones jutted out to capture the words of the famed orator. King's speech was to be broadcast on the radio and local television stations.

The gallery was packed with spectators and camp stools were placed on the House floor to provide extra seating for legislators. Representative Haynes led off with an opening prayer, followed by an introduction from House Speaker John Davoren, who was effusive in his praise.

"We are honored today by the presence of this great champion of freedom. In the unremitting struggle for social justice in America, few men have labored with greater diligence and dedication. Truly he has become the moral conscience of our nation constantly reminding us of our national heritage and ideals and prodding us to move forward to complete the unfinished work of the Republic," said Davoren.[176]

KING LAUNCHED his remarks with a nod to the irony of his invitation. "For one who has been barricaded from the seats of government and jailed so many times for attempting to petition legislatures and councils, I can assure you that this is a momentous occasion!" he said.[177]

He made it clear that he came to Massachusetts to encourage, rather than condemn, but did not mince words when it came to the issues of segregation and civil rights. "Although we have come a long, long way in the struggle for brotherhood and the struggle to make civil rights a reality for all people, I must say to you this afternoon that we have still a long, long way to go all over this nation," he said.

As examples he cited the racial discrimination found in housing, schools, and employment, whether it be the often-flagrant forms of segregation found in the South, or more subtle forms in Northern states. In either case it amounted to a "new form of slavery covered up with certain niceties of complexities," he said. "I am convinced, as I stand before you this evening, that if America and democracy are to live, segregation must die!"

In his remarks, King also stressed the importance of legislative action. He rejected the myth that addressing the nation's race relations was merely a matter of changing hearts and minds rather than laws and statutes. He weaved in references to the legacy of President John Kennedy and his work to advance civil rights and reiterated calls for a strong voting bill in Congress. He also drew attention to state-level issues such as housing and schools which were on the minds of many in his audience.

In particular, King focused on the issue of segregation, calling for an end to all segregation in public schools. "Young boys and young girls must grow up with world perspectives. Segregation debilitates the segregator as well as the segregated," he said.

In a nod to legislation pending in the Massachusetts legislature, King challenged lawmakers to do more to end housing discrimination. "Now is the time for men of goodwill to get together to make it possible for better housing conditions … for low-income and middle-income families," he said.

The soaring, sermon-like address lasted close to fifty minutes and was interrupted numerous times for applause. King closed his remarks with echoes of his past well-known speeches.

"Yes, we shall overcome! We shall overcome! We shall overcome with your help! We shall overcome because the arch of the moral universe is long, but it bends toward justice. … With this faith, we will be able to hew out of the mountain of despair, a stone of hope. With this faith, we will be able to transform the jangling discords of our nation into a beautiful symphony of brotherhood. With this faith, we will be able to speed up the day when all of God's children all over this nation, black men and white men, Jews and Gentiles, Protestants, and Catholics will be able to join hands and sing the words of the old Negro spiritual, "Free at last, free at last, thank God Almighty, we are free at last.""

Reverend Martin Luther King, Jr. gets a standing ovation as he enters the House chamber, accompanied by Secretary of State Kevin White and a contingent of state legislators. *Boston Public Library.*

The crowded House chamber erupted in applause as King concluded his speech. After the requisite flash bulbs and handshakes, King and legislative leaders were escorted out of the chamber by the sergeant-at-arms. The joint session of the legislature formally concluded at 5:20 p.m.

King's speech was also well received outside the halls of the legislature. News of his visit graced the front pages of Boston newspapers and the *Boston Globe* took note of King's homecoming in a glowing editorial, calling it "an appeal to the basic assumption upon which our entire system of government rests: that no problem remains insoluble when those of good will agree to reason together."[178]

King was scheduled to attend a Passover service at a Boston temple later that evening and the next day would feature a large-scale march and rally. For many of those in attendance though, the State House speech would remain a highlight that left an indelible memory.

Representative Dukakis, and another young legislator, Representative William Bulger of South Boston, were suitably impressed. Both recalled the speech many years later. "He was a presence that's hard to describe. He was just a very powerful presence and you felt that and sensed that," Dukakis said.[179]

Haynes, who went on to a distinguished career of his own, later called King's speech to the Massachusetts legislature a masterpiece and said it "should be read by every student of politics and every student of history."[180]

Chapter 33

VEEP VISIT VALIDATES VOLPE (1968)

"I'm not here on an arm-twisting mission."

FEBRUARY 15, 1968: It was a wintry Thursday in February when presidential candidate Richard Nixon took a break from the campaign trail in chilly New Hampshire to heat up political speculation at the Massachusetts State House.

The former vice president arrived in Boston for a $500-a-plate fundraiser at Pier Four and spent the day calling on a number of top Republicans in the state, including Governor John Volpe. At the time Nixon was leading Michigan Governor George Romney for the 1968 Republican nomination for president, with the first primary scheduled in early March.

"I'm not here on an arm-twisting mission. I have staked my fate on the primaries," Nixon told the swarm of assembled media following a closed-door meeting with Governor Volpe at the State House.[181] Volpe was on the Massachusetts presidential primary ballot as a "favorite son" candidate and thus was expected to control the state's delegates to the Republican national convention.

Following the meeting a relaxed and friendly Nixon answered questions about racial strife in U.S. cities and the nation's foreign policy in South Vietnam, but the topic on the minds of many reporters was his relationship with Governor Volpe. Was Nixon's decision to come to the Bay State and

Presidential candidate Richard Nixon's closed-door meeting with Massachusetts Governor John Volpe in the run up to the 1968 Republican presidential primary set off a firestorm of speculation. *Boston Public Library.*

visit with the popular Italian-American governor a precursor to his possible selection as a running mate?[182]

Nixon did his best to quash any vice-presidential talk, though he was effusive in his praise for his "dear friend" Volpe, who had previously served in the Eisenhower administration and had already announced he did not plan to run for re-election as governor in 1970.

"It is inappropriate and premature to talk about these matters until I become the presidential nominee," Nixon said, although he acknowledged that the Massachusetts governor "ranks high" on his list of possible vice-presidential nominees and called him a "good governor and vote-getter."[183] Volpe himself was pleased by the visit and did little to tamp down any speculation about serving in a potential Nixon administration.

Nixon's State House sojourn was enough to set the rumor mill ablaze. The visit led the Boston news and many newspapers to speculate that Volpe was now a top contender for vice president if Nixon was the Republican nominee, which looked increasingly likely. "Nixon Boosts Volpe's Hopes," wrote one Boston columnist, and the *Boston Globe* ran a front-page story about the warm relationship between the two men.

After his brief Massachusetts visit, Nixon returned to the campaign circuit in New Hampshire but the Volpe for veep speculation continued unabated. The national media soon picked up on the narrative and *Parade Magazine* published a cover story about Governor Volpe's ostensibly unstated but clear interest in the job: "Gov. John Volpe: He wants to be No. 2" read the headline, which was followed by a highly flattering piece that likened him to a Republican version of JFK.

Ultimately Nixon did choose a centrist Republican governor from an East Coast state as his vice-presidential nominee—but it was not Volpe; rather the ill-fated Spiro Agnew, governor of Maryland. Governor Volpe certainly landed on his feet, however. He was tapped to serve in the Nixon administration as the secretary of transportation and then later served as the United States ambassador to Italy.

Richard Nixon, the sitting vice-president, speaks to the State House press corps following his meeting with Governor Volpe, who harbored not-so-secret ambitions to serve in the same role on a Nixon presidential ticket. *Boston Public Library.*

Chapter 34

STUDENT PROTESTERS SWARM STATE HOUSE (1970)

*One, two, three, four, we don't want
your f-------- war!*

MAY 5, 1970: Thousands of students descended on the State House in early May for an anti-war protest in the wake of the United States' recent invasion of Cambodia. The peace rally had been planned for several days, but passions were further inflamed by the slaying of four unarmed college students in Ohio one day earlier.

Many students marched on foot to the State House from area college campuses. The swelling crowds, estimated between ten and twenty thousand, spilled over onto Boston

The State House was the scene of a massive rally following the escalation of operations into Cambodia. Chanting anti-war slogans, protesters took over and occupied the lawn for five hours before eventually dispersing peacefully. *UPI.*

Common and along Beacon Street where a microphone stand and makeshift stage were hastily set up.

Chants of "Peace now!" and "One, two, three, four, we don't want your -f------- war," rippled through the placard-filled throng.

The protestors eventually broke through a security perimeter and took over the front lawn of the capitol building. Police locked down the main doorway and executive offices of the State House and fanned out along the street in riot gear, but otherwise did not attempt to block the student protest.

A number of legislators watched the unfolding scene from the third-floor balcony outside the Senate chamber and a few ventured out into the crowd.

Student protestors mounted and rang the two-thousand-pound Liberty Bell located in front of the State House during the demonstration. The bronze replica was gifted to the state in 1950 as part of a national savings bond campaign. Today the bell is housed inside Doric Hall. *Boston Public Library.*

Students swarm the State House steps in 1970, one day after the Kent State shootings. *University of Massachusetts at Amherst Special Collections.*

They included Senate President Maurice Donahue who stood in short-sleeves with a microphone and addressed the students sprawled on the grass.

Donahue was sharply critical of President Nixon's "quicksand policies" in Vietnam and advocated for an anti-war referendum question. He had made no formal announcement as of yet, but Donahue was also expected to be a candidate for governor that fall.

"We have learned that confrontation with limitations doesn't work—that in our society it is dangerous in the extreme to involve ourselves in a war that the majority of the people do not support," Donahue said.[184] The students may have been sympathetic to the message, but they did not seem overly enthusiastic to hear the messenger, nor any political leader, and Donahue received only tepid applause.

At one point, protesters demanded that the State House flags be ordered to half-mast in memory of fallen soldiers and the four students slain by National Guardsmen at Kent State University. A few ambitious students even attempted to scale the flagpoles themselves. Others tried to ring the Liberty Bell replica on the front steps of the State House.

The pressure to lower the flags intensified as the rally continued past midday. Governor Francis Sargent eventually relented and gave the order to lower the flags to half-mast. Applause erupted as the capitol police began untying the rope, and then, as the American flag was lowered, the crowd went quiet—for the first time that day.

Governor Sargent was later criticized for agreeing to the protestors' demands, but he defended his action given the "highly explosive" nature of the event. He later offered praise for police officials for keeping the peace, as well as the protestors themselves, given that "no ambulances had to be called and there was no bloodshed."[185]

A NOTE ON SOURCES

Newspapers represent the first rough draft of history: it's an aphorism that my father often shared with me, and it certainly ring true here. I relied on a number of primary source materials for this project, but it would not have been possible without access to the many newspapers covering this time period—generally 1798 to 1970. I relied extensively on the archives of the *Boston Globe, Boston Herald, Springfield Republican* and earlier publications, including the *Liberator, Boston Gazette, Boston Courier,* and *Boston Evening Transcript,* among others. The Boston Public Library is an excellent source for a range of newspaper and periodicals. I also relied on Google news archive, genealogybank.com, newspapers.com, newspaperarchive.com, Accessible Archives, the Massachusetts State Library, the Library of Congress, and Hathi Trust Digital Library. The collections of Digital Commonwealth, particularly their image archives, were also invaluable. A bibliography and specific reference notes are cited in the source notes that follow. These represent an abridged version of sources used in this narrative to give credit to other authors, secondary sources and compiled collections of primary sources.

SELECTED BIBLIOGRAPHY

Andrews, George F. *State Government, 1886: Biography of Members, Councillor, House and Senate Committees, State* House Directory, Department Commission and Clerical Register. Compiled from Sergeant-at-Arms Office. Boston. 1886 and 1887.

Barnes, Gilbert H., and Dwight L. Dumond, eds. *Letters of Theodore Dwight Weld, Angelina Grimké Weld, and Sarah Grimké, 1822–1844.* 2 vols. The American Historical Association, The Albert J. Beveridge Memorial Fund. New York: D. Appleton-Century Company, 1934.

Beatty, Jack. *The Rascal King: The Life and Times of James Michael Curley (1874-1958).* New York: Addison Wesley Publishing Company, 1992.

Beecher, Catharine E. *An Essay on Slavery and Abolitionism, with Reference to the Duty of American Females.* 2nd ed. Philadelphia: Henry Perkins; Perkins & Marvin, Boston, 1837.

Birney, Catherine H. *The Grimké Sisters: Sarah and Angelina Grimké, the First American Women Advocates of Abolition and Woman's Rights.* Philadelphia: C. T. Dillingham, 1885.

Burrill, Ellen M. *The State House*, Wright and Potter Printing Co., 1912.

Butt, Archibald Willingham. *Taft and Roosevelt: The Intimate Letters of Archie Butt.* 2 vols. Garden City, NY: Doubleday, Doran & Company, Inc., 1930.

The Bulfinch State House, 1798-1898. Bulfinch State House Centennial Committee. Boston: Wright & Potter Printing Company, 1898.

Cellem, Robert. *Visit of His Royal Highness the Prince of Wales to the British North American Provinces and United States in the Year 1860.* Toronto: Henry Rowsell, 1861

Chace, James. *1912: Wilson, Roosevelt, Taft and Debs—The Election that Changed the Country*. New York: Simon & Schuster, 2009.

Chaplin, Jane Dunbar. *The Life of Charles Sumner*. Boston: D. Lothrop & Co.; Dover, NH: G. T. Day & Co, 1874.

Commonwealth of Massachusetts. *Interim Report of the Special Commission on Communism, Subversive Activities and Related Matters within the Commonwealth*. Boston, 1955.

Dalton, Cornelius, John Wirkkala, and Anne Thomas. *Leading the Way: A History of the Massachusetts General Court, 1629–1980*. Boston: Office of the Massachusetts Secretary of State, 1984.

Dix, Dorothea Lynde. *Memorial. To the Legislature of Massachusetts protesting against the confinement of insane persons and idiots in almshouses and prisons*. Boston, Printed by Munroe & Francis, 1843.

Hennessy, Michael E. *Twenty-Five Years of Massachusetts Politics: From Russell to McCall, 1890-1915*. Foreword by Henry Cabot Lodge. Boston: Boston, 1917.

Hopkins, Pauline E. "Famous Men of the Negro Race." *The Colored American Magazine*, March 1901.

Irwin Richard W. *A History of the Emblem of the Codfish in the Hall of the House of Representatives*. Boston: Wright and Potter Printing Co., State Printers, 1895.

Jenkins, Candace. *State House Historic Structure Report*, Ann Beha Associates, Society for the Preservation of New England Antiquities. Vol. 1, 1985.

Keller, Helen. *The Story of My Life*. New York: Doubleday, Page & Co., 1903.

Kenneally, James, "I Want to Go to Jail": The Woman's Party Reception for President Wilson in Boston, 1919, Historical Journal of Massachusetts, Vol. 45, Winter 2017.

King, Martin Luther, Jr. The Autobiography of Martin Luther King, Jr. Edited by Clayborne Carson. New York: Warner Books, 1998.

Kopel, Jonathan. "President William Howard Taft's Trowel: Spreading the Cementing of Unity and Tolerance in Public Health." *Journal of Community Hospital Internal Medicine Perspectives*, 2021.

Lachevre, Susan G. *Art of the Civil War at the Massachusetts State House*. Massachusetts Art Commission, 2012.

Lerner, Gerda. *The Grimké Sisters from South Carolina: Pioneers for Women's Rights and Abolition*. Chapel Hill: University of North Carolina Press, 2004.

Massachusetts General Court. House of Representatives. *Committee on History of the Emblem of the Codfish*, Ernest William Roberts, James A. Gallivan.

Massachusetts General Court. *Manual for the Use of the General Court Containing the Rules and Orders of the Two Branches, Together with the Constitution of the Commonwealth, and that of the United States.* Boston, Wright & Potter, 1867.

McMaster, John Bach. *Daniel Webster.* New York: D. Appleton & Co., 1902.

National Park Service. *Founders and Frontiersmen: The Early History of the Massachusetts State House.* Washington, D.C.: National Park Service, 1960.

Parker. John F. *Legislative Life, its Realities, Facts, Wit & Humor,* State House, Boston, January 1985.

Pearson, Henry Greenleaf. *The Life of John A. Andrew, Governor of Massachusetts, 1861-1865,* Houghton Mifflin, 1904.

Records of the Governor and Company of the Massachusetts Bay in New England. Printed by order of the legislature. Edited by Nathaniel B. Shurtleff. Vol. I, 1628-1641. Boston: Press of William White, Printer to the Commonwealth, 1853.

Rugg, Arthur P. *A Famous Colonial Litigation: The Case Between Richard Sherman and Capt. Robert Keayne,* American Antiquarian Society. 1920.

Seabrook, Nick. *One Person, One Vote: A Surprising History of Gerrymandering in America,* Pantheon Books, 2022.

Shlaes, Amity. *Coolidge.* Harper Collins, 2013.

Sobel, Robert. *Coolidge, An American Enigma,* Regnery Publishing, 1998.

Stevens, Doris. *Jailed for Freedom.* New York: Liveright Publishing Corporation, 1920.

Sumner, William H. *Memoir of Increase Sumner, Governor of Massachusetts: Together with a Genealogy of the Sumner Family.* Boston: New England Historic Genealogical Society, 1854.

Taft, William H. *William H. Taft Papers: Series 3: General Correspondence and Related Material, 1877 to 1941; 1920 M-Z.* 1920. Library of Congress.

Tiffany, Francis. *Life of Dorothea Lynde Dix.* Boston: Houghton, Mifflin and Co. 1890.

Turner, Edward R. *Calvin, Coolidge: A Man of Vision--not a Visionary.* 1925.

Washburn, Robert. M. *Calvin Coolidge; His First Biography;* Small, Maynard and Company, 1923.

West, John. *Boston Directory:* Manning and Loring, 1796 and 1798.

Winthrop, John, 1588-1649. *Winthrop's Journal: History of New England, 1630-1649.* New York: Barnes & Noble, 1966.

INDEX

A

Adams, Sam, 14
Agnew, Spiro, 152
Allen, Frank, 99, 124
Andrew, John, 41, 42, 43
Apted, Charles, 103

B

Banks, Nathaniel, 37
Bates, John, 55, 124
Bligh, Thomas, 103
Bolling, Royal, 144
Boston Common, 38, 42, 81, 84, 89, 121,
    145, 154
Bowker, Philip, 130, 133
Bradford, Robert, 114
Brockton, 78, 79, 80, 81, 83
Bulfinch, Charles, 13
Bulger, William, 149
Butler, Benjamin, 122, 123
Byrd, Richard, 99

C

Cape Cod, 51, 102
Caples, Richard, 139

Civil War, 30, 36, 41, 42, 43, 44, 46, 48,
    75, 76, 77, 86, 165
Collins, John, 128, 129
Communist Party, 131, 132, 133
Coolidge, Calvin, 66, 67, 69, 70, 89, 124
Corrigan, Douglas, 98
Couch, Darius, 43
Cox, Channing, 76, 124
Curley, James, 108, 115, 117, 125
Cushing, Grafton, 57

D

Davoren, John, 146
Dever, Paul, 117, 121
Dix, Dorothea, 26, 27, 29, 30
Donahue, Maurice, 155
Donaldson, Sylvia, 78, 79, 81, 82, 83
Dorgon, Thomas, 108
Doric Hall, 37, 43
Dukakis, Michael, 126, 144, 149

E

Earhart, Amelia, 95, 96
Elder, Ruth, 98
Ely, Joseph, 96

F

Farnum, Ralph, 39
Federalist Party, 18, 19, 21
Fillmore, Millard, 30
Fitzgerald, John, 62
Fitzgerald, Susan, 81, 84, 85
Fuller, Alvan, 97
Furculo, Foster, 127

G

Gardner, Henry, 32
Garrison, William Lloyd, 24, 35, 46
Gerry, Elbridge, 18, 19, 20, 21
Gerrymander, 20
Gleason, Jackie, 134, 135
Greenwood, Levi, 63, 66
Grimké, Angela, 22, 23, 25
Grimké, Sarah, 24
Guild, Curtis, 124

H

Hall of Flags, 76, 86, 90, 98, 117, 143
Hammond, Watson, 49, 50, 51
Harrington, Kevin, 144
Harvard Lampoon, 102, 104, 105
Hawthorne, William, 91
Haynes, Michael, 144, 146
Hearst Jr., William, 130
Herter, Christian, 125
Howe, Samuel Gridley, 27, 30
Hull, John, 78
Hurley, Charles, 125

K

Keayne, Robert, 91
Keller, Helen, 52, 53, 54, 55
Kennedy, John, 137, 138, 143
King, Martin Luther, 38, 39, 144, 145,
146, 147, 149, 159, 160

L

Lenroot, Irving, 70
Liberator, The, 24, 25, 33, 35, 46
Liberty Bell, 155
Lincoln, Abraham, 77, 86, 87

M

MacArthur, Douglas, 116, 117, 119, 120
Martha's Vineyard, 50
Mashpee, 49, 51
Massachusetts Commission for the
    Blind, 55
McCamant, Wallace, 70
McCarthy, Joseph, 132
Memorial Hall, 43
Mitchell, Charles, 44, 45, 47
Morey, Agnes, 73

N

Nixon, Richard, 150, 151, 152

O

Old State House, 13, 101

P

Pankhurst, Sylvia, 85
Peabody, Endicott, 126
Perkins School for the Blind, 52
Phillips, Wendell, 46, 47
Pierce, Franklin, 34
Plunkett, Thomas, 41
Plymouth, 22, 28
Powers, John, 131
Prince of Wales, 37, 39, 40, 159

R

Reeb, James, 145
Revere, Paul, 14
Robinson, George, 123
Romney, George, 150
Romney, Mitt, 126
Roosevelt, Theodore, 56, 58, 60, 61, 62, 64
Russell, William, 123

S

Sacred Cod, 100, 102, 103, 104, 105
Saltonstall, Leverett, 112, 113, 125
Sergeant, Francis, 105
Sherman, Elizabeth, 91, 93
Simmon, Edward, 43
Skerry, Michael, 130
Smith, John James, 47
State House dome, 22, 25, 42, 113
Sullivan, Anne, 53

Sumner, Charles, 27, 30, 31, 32, 33, 35, 39
Sumner, Increase, 13, 14, 15
Swift, Jane, 126

T

Taft, William, 61, 62, 63, 64, 69
Thacher, Peter, 15
Thompson, John, 139
Truman, Harry, 118, 120

V

Volpe, John, 126, 138, 145, 150

W

Walker, Edwin, 44, 45, 46
Wampanoag, 50, 90
Wilson, Woodrow, 72, 73, 74
Winthrop, John, 89, 93, 141

ENDNOTES

Chapter 1 notes

[1] *Boston Price Current and Intelligencer*, January 11, 1798, 4. See also West. *Boston Directory*, 1796, 1798.
[2] Jenkins, *State House*; Burrill, *State House.*
[3] "New State House," *North American* (Philadelphia*)*, January 18, 1798, 3.
[4] *Columbia Gazette*, January 13, 1798, 2.
[5] *New Hampshire Gazette*, January 24, 1798, 2.
[6] *Boston Gazette*, January 22, 1798, 2.
[7] *Journals of the General Court*, Vol. 18, May 1797 to March 1798, State Library of Massachusetts.

Chapter 2 notes

[8] This Republican Party, often referred to as the Democratic-Republican Party, bears no direct relation to our modern-day Republican Party, which originated just before the Civil War. The Democratic-Republican were an offshoot of the Anti-Federalist movement, popularized by Thomas Jefferson. We use the term "Republican" here since that was the customary usage of the time.
[9] Seabrook, *One Person.*
[10] *Boston Gazette*, February 24, 1812, 1.
[11] Ibid.
[12] *Boston Gazette*, March 26, 1812, 2.
[13] Ibid.

Chapter 3 notes

[14] Grimké's name is sometimes spelled without the trailing accent, which is a legacy of her French ancestry. She used the accent in most of her written letters and that has been the preferred reference in most historical accounts. Grimké was married several months after her speech to the legislature and went by Angela Grimké Weld.

[15] Birney, *The Grimke Sisters*, 228. See also Lerner, *Grimké*, 1-12.

[16] *Liberator*, March 2, 1838, 3. See also *Springfield Republican*, February 24, 1838, 2; and *Boston Gazette* as published *in New York Journal of Commerce*, February 24, 1838.

[17] "Letter from Boston," *Hampshire Gazette*, February 28, 1838, 3.

[18] *Liberator*, March 2, 1838, 3.

[19] *Liberator*, March 9, 1838, 3; *The Daily Atlas* (Boston), March 3, 1838, 2.

[20] "Miss Grimke," *Boston Reformer*, as published in *Liberator*, March 9, 1838, 2.

[21] Letter from Angelina Grimké to Sarah M. Douglas, February 25, 1838, as published in Barnes, *Letters*.

Chapter 4 notes

[22] Tiffany, *Life, 76.*

[23] Dix, *Memorial*, 4-7.

[24] Ibid, 9.

[25] Ibid, 22.

[26] Ibid, 32.

[27] *Salem Register*, January 30, 1843, 2.

[28] *Franklin Democrat,* February 14, 1843, 2.

[29] *Christian Register*, January 28, 1843, 3; *Boston Recorder*, January 26, 1843, 14.

Chapter 5 notes

[30] *Liberator*, November 7, 1856, p. 2. See also *Lowell Daily Citizen*, October 31, 1856; *National Aegis*, November 12, 1856, 1; *Salem Register*, November 3, 1856, 2; and *Saturday Evening Gazette*, November 8, 1856, 4.

[31] Letter to John Bigelow, October 9, 1856, as published by Chaplin, *Life of Charles Sumner*.

[32] *Liberator*, November 7, 1856, 2.

[33] *Berkshire County Eagle*, November 7, 1856.

[34] *Hartford Courant*, December 8, 1856, 2.

Chapter 6 notes

[35] The unveiling was originally held on September 17, 1859, but due to bad weather the ceremony had to be moved inside. A repeat performance was held outside on September 27, 1859.

[36] *Liberator*, September 9, 1859, 2.

[37] *Liberator*, October 21, 1859, 1, quoting Washington newspaper.

Chapter 7 notes

[38] *Boston Courier*, October 22, 1860, 1. See also Rowsell, *Visit,* 408-418.

[39] *Salem Register*, October 22, 1860, 6.

[40] *Liberator*, November 2, 1860, 4.

[41] Ibid.

[42] *Salem Register*, October 22, 1860, 6.

Chapter 8 notes

[43] *Boston Herald*, December 23, 1865, 4.

[44] Ibid.

[45] Pearson, *Life,* 254-258.

[46] *Daily Evening News* (Fall River), December 23, 1865, 2.

[47] See Lachevre, *Art of the Civil War,* 30-31; *Boston Post,* May 29, 1902, 7; and *Boston Globe*, May 30, 1902, 7.

Chapter 9 notes

[48] In many newspaper accounts Walker's first name was listed as Edward.

[49] Massachusetts General Court. *Manual, 1867.*

[50] *Springfield Republican*, November 7, 1866, 6.

[51] *Boston Evening Traveller*, November 7, 1866, 2.

[52] *Springfield Republican*, November 8, 1866, 2.

[53] *Boston Herald*, November 7, 1866, 2.

[54] For election details, see *Boston Daily Advertiser*, November 7, 1867, 2; *Boston Herald*, November 7, 1867, 2; *Boston Post*, November 7, 1867, 4; and *Springfield Republican*, November 6, 1867, 4.

[55] See also *Black Legislators in the Massachusetts General Court 1867- Present,* State Library of Massachusetts. Boston, 2010.

Chapter 10 notes

[56] *Barnstable Patriot*, September 1, 1885, 2.

[57] For election details see *Barnstable Patriot*, November 10, 1885, 2; and *Boston Globe*, November 11, 1885, 8.

[58] His patent is duly registered with the United States Patent and Trademark Office, #280372.

[59] *Barnstable Patriot*, January 2, 1886, 2.

[60] Massachusetts General Court. *Manual, 1886, 1887* and *Journal of the House*, June 1886.

[61] *Boston Globe*, May 4, 1886, 3.

[62] *Worcester Evening Gazette*, May 4, 1886, p 6.

Chapter 11 notes

[63] See hearing details generally in *Fall River Globe*, March 7, 1903, 5; *Berkshire Eagle*, March 20, 1903. 2; *Boston Globe*, March 6, 1903, 1; *Worcester Daily Spy*, March 7, 1903, 1.

[64] *Boston Herald*, March 7, 1903, 7.

[65] *Boston Evening Transcript*, March 7, 1903,18; *Berkshire Eagle*, March 20, 1903, 2; and *Boston Globe*, March 7, 1903, 14.

[66] *Massachusetts Commission for the Blind History*. Mass.gov. Accessed July 30, 2024, https://www.mass.gov/info-details/massachusetts-commission-for-the-blind-history-0.

Chapter 12 notes

[67] *Boston Journal*, February 27, 1912, 1.

[68] See *Journal of the House*, February 1912; *Boston Journal*, February 27, 1912,

[69] "Roosevelt Answers Cry of Revolution," *New York Times*, February 27, 1912, 1-3. Speech also published in *Boston Globe*, February 27, 1912, 4.

[70] *Boston Evening Transcript*, February 26, 1912, 1.

[71] *Boston Globe*, February 27, 1912, 5.

Chapter 13 notes

[72] Taft, *Papers*. 235.

[73] Butt, *Taft and Roosevelt;* and Kopel, *Taft's Trowel,* 880-882.

[74] *Boston Evening Transcript*, March 18, 1912, 5.

[75] *Boston Globe*, March 18, 1912, 2; and *Holyoke Transcript*, March 19, 1912, 7.

[76] *Boston Journal*, March 19, 1912, 4.

[77] *Boston Herald*, March 19, 1912, 3.

[78] *Boston Evening Transcript*, March 18, 1912, 5.

[79] Taft did later edge Roosevelt to win the Republican nomination, but it came at a cost. The bitter primary contributed to Roosevelt launching a third party bid as a "Bull Moose" Progressive and Democrat Woodrow Wilson ended up winning the 1912 presidential election in a landslide.

Chapter 14 notes

[80] Autobiography of Calvin Coolidge, as published in *Rochester Journal*, January 31, 1933, 12.
[81] Ibid.
[82] Ibid.
[83] As quoted in Sobel, *Coolidge*, 103.
[84] Coolidge Foundation. "Coolidge Chronology." Accessed June 26, 2024. https://coolidgefoundation.org/presidency/coolidge-chronology-8/.

Chapter 15 notes

[85] "To Burn Wilson's Speech on Common," *Boston Globe*, February 24, 1919, 9; and Kenneally, *I Want to Go to Jail*, 106-108.
[86] *Fall River Evening News*, February 24, 1919, 1; and *Fitchburg Sentinel*, February 24, 1919, 1.
[87] Stevens, *Jailed for Freedom*, 322.
[88] Ibid.

Chapter 16 notes

[89] *Boston Globe*, August 15, 1924, 4.
[90] *Boston Globe*, August 11, 1924, 6.
[91] *Boston Herald*, August 11, 1924, 3.
[92] The last surviving member was Albert H. Woolson of Duluth, Minnesota, who served as a drummer and bugler in the Union Army and died in 1956 at the age of 106. For the 1924 Boston encampment records see *Journal of the Fifty-Eighth National Encampment of the Grand Army of the Republic*. Boston: Government Printing Office, 1925. See also GAR records by year: http://www.garrecords.org/

Chapter 17 notes

[93] Since 1879, Massachusetts women were able to vote in local school committee elections.

94 The town of North Bridgewater became the town of Brockton (later city) in the spring of 1874. The names Avon and Allerton were also considered, but Brockton won out. See *Boston Post*, May 5, 1874, 3.

95 *Boston Globe*, January 9, 1929, 24.

96 *Springfield Republican*, February 19, 1922, 1.

97 *New Britain Herald*, February 22, 1926, 12.

98 *Fort Worth Star Telegram*, February 24, 1926, 1.

99 *Quincy Patriot Ledger*, September 8, 1926, 3.

100 *Boston Herald*, October 8, 1926, 8.

101 *Boston Globe*, June 16, 1930, 29.

102 *Boston Journal*, February 24, 1911, p. 3.

103 *Boston Evening Transcript,* February 24, 1911, 3

104 Ibid.

Chapter 18 notes

105 *Boston Herald*, February 17, 1928, 1.

106 "Rev. L.H. Caswell, Resembled Lincoln; Noted Impersonator, Ex-Pastor Here, Dies in Connecticut," *New York Times*, October 14, 1939, 19.

107 *Worcester Evening Gazette*, June 9, 1934, 6.

Chapter 19 notes

108 This was the first session held on Massachusetts soil. The royal charter was granted in 1629 in England. See Dalton, *Leading*, 4-5.

109 *Boston Herald*, October 21, 1930, 13.

110 *Boston Globe*, December 15, 1928, 12.

111 "A Model of Christian Charity," April 1630 sermon written or delivered aboard the *Arabella*, is widely attributed to John Winthrop, though the authorship has been the subject of some scholarly debate.

112 *Boston Globe*, December 31, 1930, 20.

113 Ibid.

114 Massachusetts Historical Society. *Papers of the Winthrop Family*, Volume 4, 1642-07-15.

115 Rugg, *Famous Colonial Litigation.*

116 Massachusetts Historical Society. *Papers of the Winthrop Family*, Volume 4, 1642-07-15.

117 Winthrop, John. *Winthrop's Journal, "History of New England," 1630-1649: Volume 2.* 119.

Chapter 20 notes

[118] *Boston Herald*, June 30, 1932, 2.
[119] Ibid.
[120] "Ruth Elder Stopped All Work at City Hall for a Half-Hour," *Boston Globe*, March 6, 1928, 14.
[121] *Boston Globe*, August 5, 1938, 5.

Chapter 21 notes

[122] Massachusetts General Court, *A history of the emblem.*
[123] *Boston Globe*, April 28, 1933.
[124] *Boston Herald*, April 28, 1933, 5.
[125] As republished in *Buffalo Evening News*, May 3, 1933, 8.
[126] *Boston Globe*, November 16, 1968, 5.
[127] *Boston Record American*, November 17, 1968, 26.
[128] Ibid.

Chapter 22 notes

[129] *Boston Globe*, October 3, 1935, 3.
[130] *Springfield Weekly Republican*, June 27, 1935, 3.
[131] See *Joseph Pedlosky vs. Massachusetts Institute of Technology*, 352 Mass. 127.

Chapter 23 notes

[132] *Worcester Palladium*, May 9, 1849, 2.
[133] *Daily Transcript*, May 22, 1855, 2.
[134] *Springfield Daily Republican*, July 18, 1900.
[135] *Sunday Herald*, June 29, 1902, 21.

Chapter 24 notes

[136] *Boston Globe*, October 5, 1942, 8.
[137] *Springfield Daily Republican*, February 27, 1942, 7.
[138] *Boston Globe*, October 8, 1942, 32.

Chapter 25 notes

[139] *Boston Globe*, May 20, 1947, 24. See also *Athol Daily News*, January 3, 1947, 1; and *Lynn Daily Item*, May 21, 1947, 1.

Chapter 26 notes

[140] *Boston Daily Globe*, July 26, 1951, 1.
[141] For national reaction, see "The General Goes to Boston," *Time Magazine*, August 6, 1951.
[142] *Boston Record American*, September 12, 1963, 30.
[143] *Springfield Union*, September 12, 1963, 17.

Chapter 27 notes

[144] *Springfield Daily Republican*, January 4, 1884, 4.
[145] *Lowell Sun*, January 5, 1884, 8.
[146] *Boston Globe*, January 7, 1887, 8.
[147] *Boston Morning Journal*, January 5, 1894, 5.
[148] *Boston Globe*, January 8, 1903, 8.
[149] *Boston Globe*, January 6, 1905, 7.
[150] *Boston Globe*, January 7, 1909, 4.
[151] *Holyoke Transcript-Telegram*, January 9, 1931, 12.
[152] *Boston Globe*, January 3, 2003, 26.

Chapter 28 notes

[153] *Boston Daily Record*, February 3, 1954, 5.
[154] Ibid.
[155] Ibid.

Chapter 29 notes

[156] *Boston Evening American*, 4/1/1955, p. 3.
[157] *Boston Daily Record*, 4/1/1955, p. 20.
[158] *Lynn Daily Item*, June 9, 1955, 1.
[159] *Interim Report of the Special Commission on Communism, Subversive Activities and Related Matters within the Commonwealth*, June 1955, Wright and Potter Printing Co., 16.
[160] Ibid.
[161] *Boston Globe*, June 9, 1955, 1.
[162] Ibid.
[163] *Berkshire Eagle*, January 24, 1956, 14.

[164] *Thirteenth Report of the Special Commission on Communism, Subversive Activities and Related Matters within the Commonwealth*; Wright and Potter Printing Co., January 1960.
[165] See Massachusetts General Laws, Chapter 264, § 16A and 17.

Chapter 30 notes

[166] *Boston Herald*, September 9,1959, 12.
[167] *Holyoke Daily Transcript*, September 10, 1959, 10.

Chapter 31 notes

[168] "Squeals Greet Guest," *Boston Globe*, January 10, 1961, 11.
[169] "John F. Kennedy Shuns Speech by Famous Namesake," *Berkshire Eagle*, January 10, 1961, 10. See also: James V. Horrigan, "All about the 'Other' JFK," *Commonwealth Magazine*, August 1, 2004.
[170] "State House Talk Seen as Call for Moral Uplift in Bay State," *Boston Globe*, January 10, 1961, 11.
[171] Kennedy's speech as delivered differed slightly from his prepared remarks. The former is republished here.
[172] Letter of January 6. 1961. Papers of John F. Kennedy. Presidential Papers. President's Office Files. Speech Files. *Address to Massachusetts State Legislature*, January 9, 1961. Note: Letter is identified as being "from the President-elect to an unknown recipient," but it is clearly addressed to Kennedy.
[173] "The Presidency: The 35th," *Time Magazine*, January 27, 1961. In retrospect Kennedy needn't have worried. His inaugural address, delivered on January 20, 1961, would long be remembered, including his now famous call to action: "ask not what your country can do for you—ask what you can do for your country."

Chapter 32 notes

[174] "Martin Luther King's Boston Ties Remembered," WBUR, January 16, 2012, www.wbur.org/news/2012/01/16/mlk-boston. Accessed June 25, 2024.
[175] *Boston Globe*, April 14, 1965, 1.
[176] Governor Davoren remarks and Dr. King address later published as H.4155, Wright & Potter Printing Co., May 3, 1965, State Library of Massachusetts, accessed at https://archives.lib.state.ma.us/handle/2452/70100.
[177] Ibid.
[178] *Boston Globe*, April 23, 1965.
[179] "Martin Luther King's Boston Ties Remembered," WBUR, January 16, 2012, www.wbur.org/news/2012/01/16/mlk-boston. Accessed June 26, 2024.

[180] WUMB, interview with Reverend Haynes, January 21, 1986, americanarchive.org/catalog/cpb-aacip_345-171vhk97, Accessed June 25, 2024.

Chapter 33 notes

[181] *Boston Globe*, February 16, 1968, 1.
[182] See also *Boston Herald Traveler*, February 16, 1968, 16; and *Boston Record American*, February 16, 1968, 5.
[183] *Boston Globe*, February 16, 1968, 1.

Chapter 34 notes

[184] *Boston Globe*, May 5, 1970, 2.
[185] *Patriot Ledger*, May 6, 1970, 1.

ABOUT THE AUTHOR

Josh S. Cutler, a native of Duxbury, Massachusetts, is a former state legislator, attorney, and newspaper editor who spent more than a decade working under the Golden Dome. Cutler is a graduate of Skidmore College, Suffolk University Law School, and the University of Massachusetts at Dartmouth (M.A., environmental policy). He is also the author of *Mobtown Massacre: Alexander Hanson and the Newspaper War of 1812* (History Press, 2019), and *The Boston Gentlemen's Mob: Maria Chapman and the Abolition Riot of 1835* (History Press, 2021). For author website, speaker requests, and contact information, please visit: www.joshscutler.com.

www.ingramcontent.com/pod-product-compliance
Lightning Source LLC
Chambersburg PA
CBHW041202150726
48006CB00016B/2073